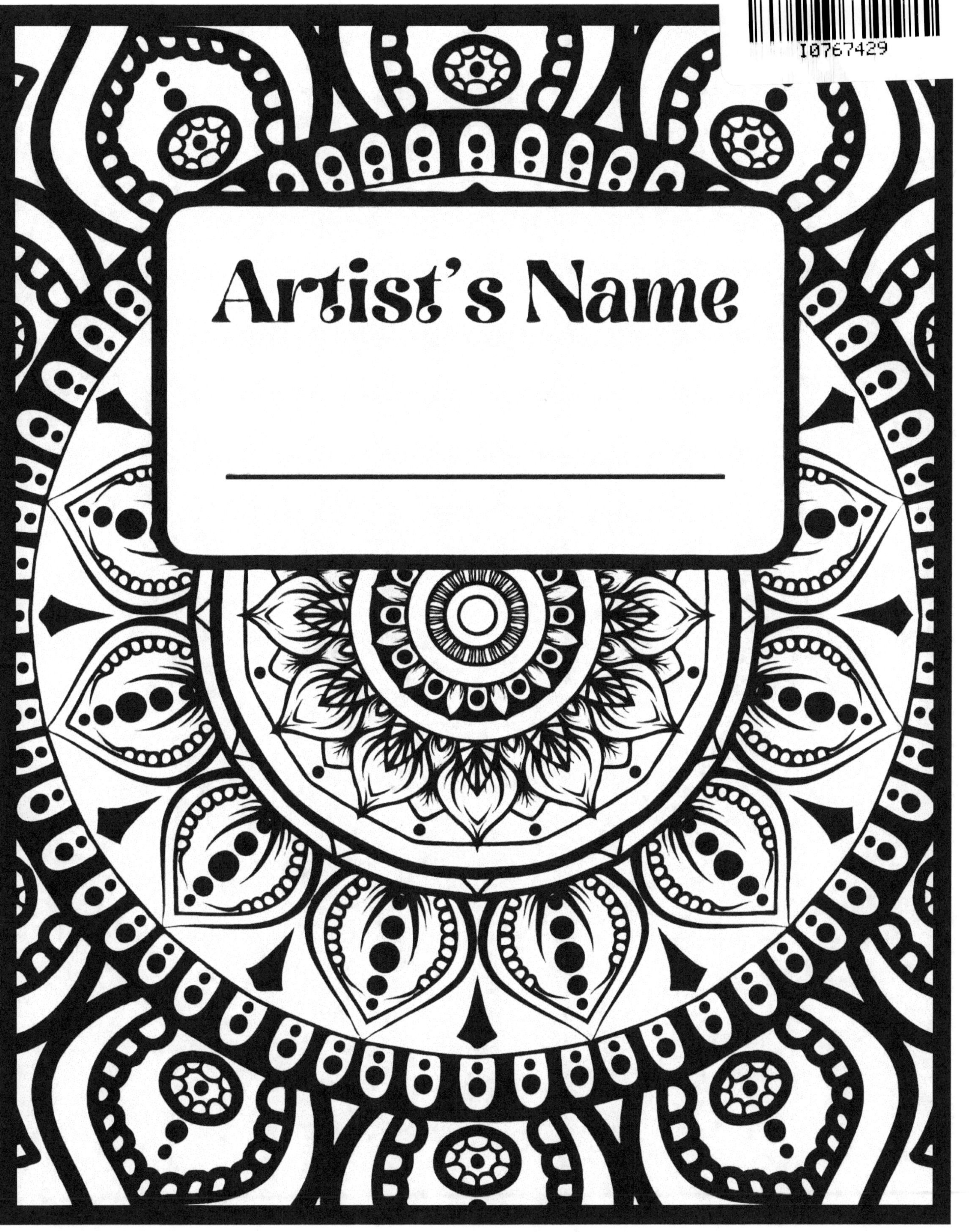
Artist's Name

Color Testing Page

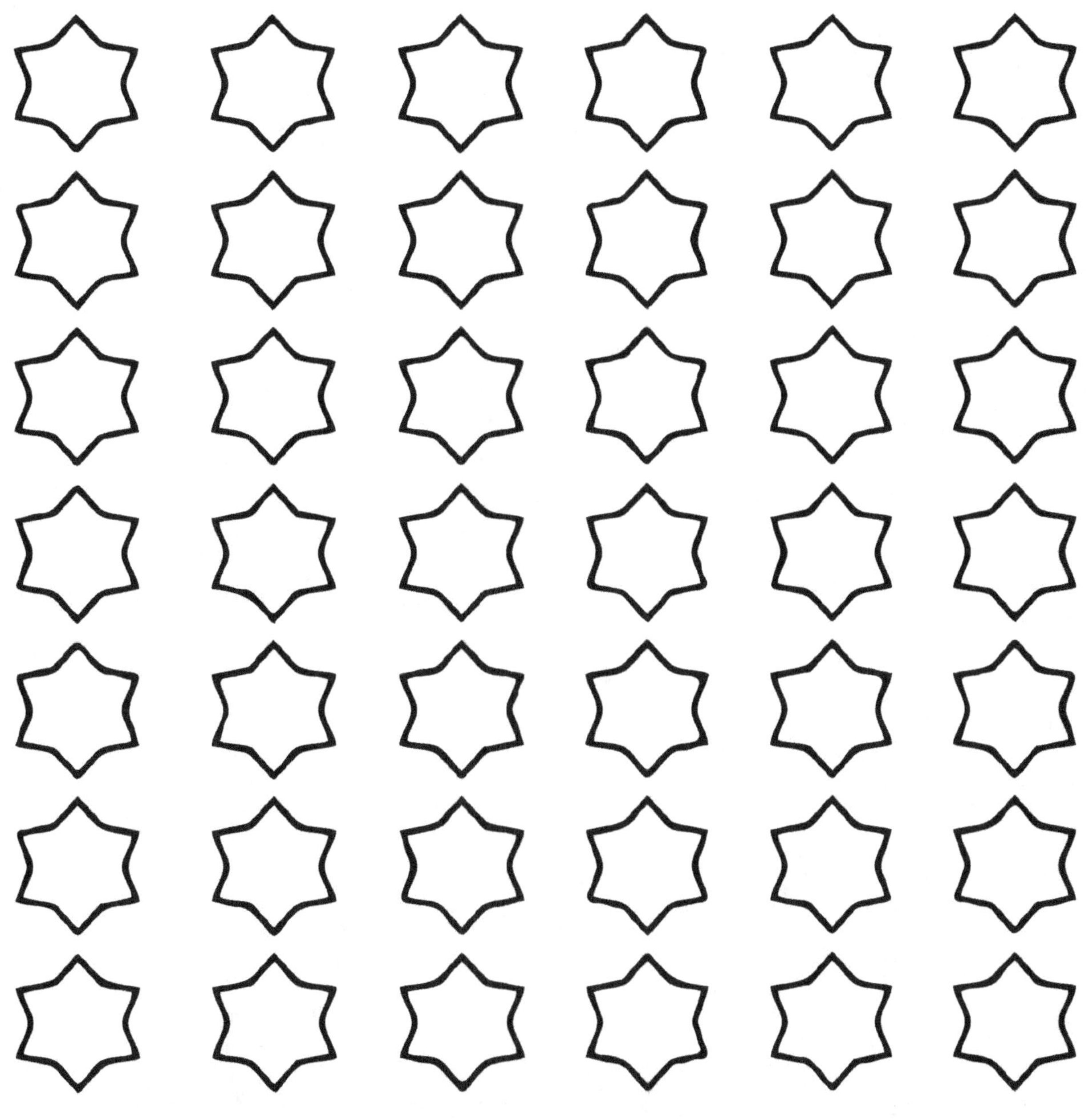

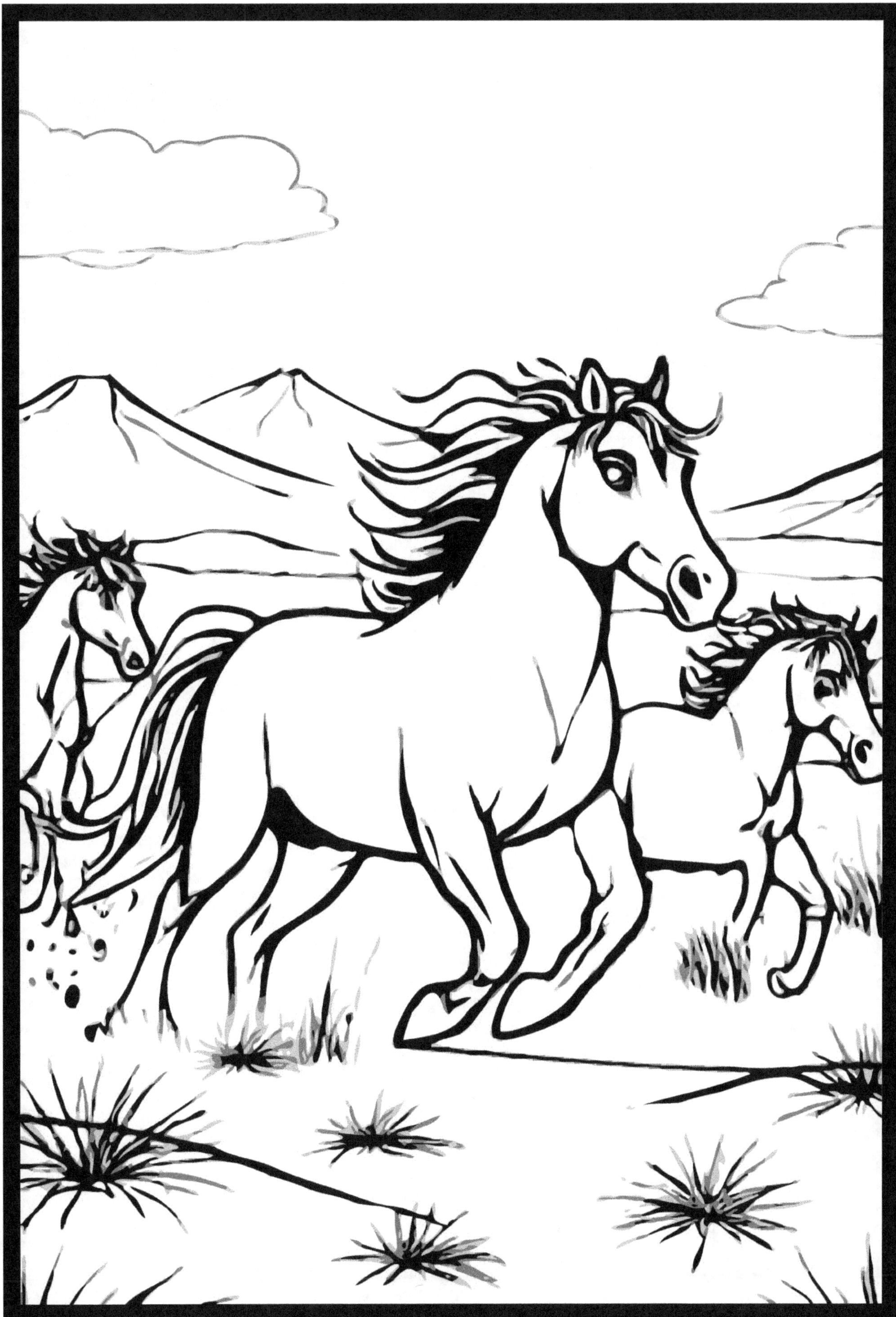

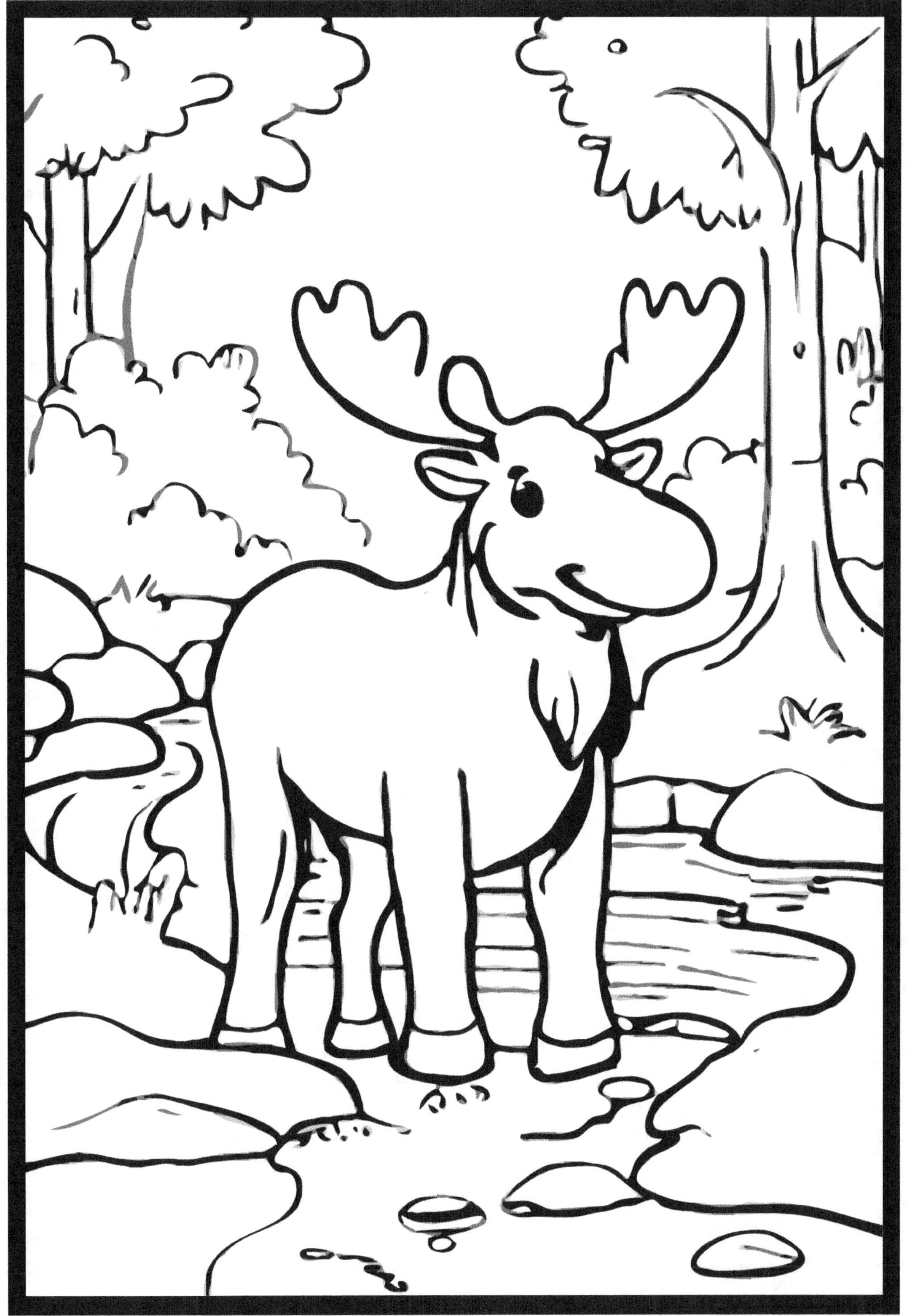

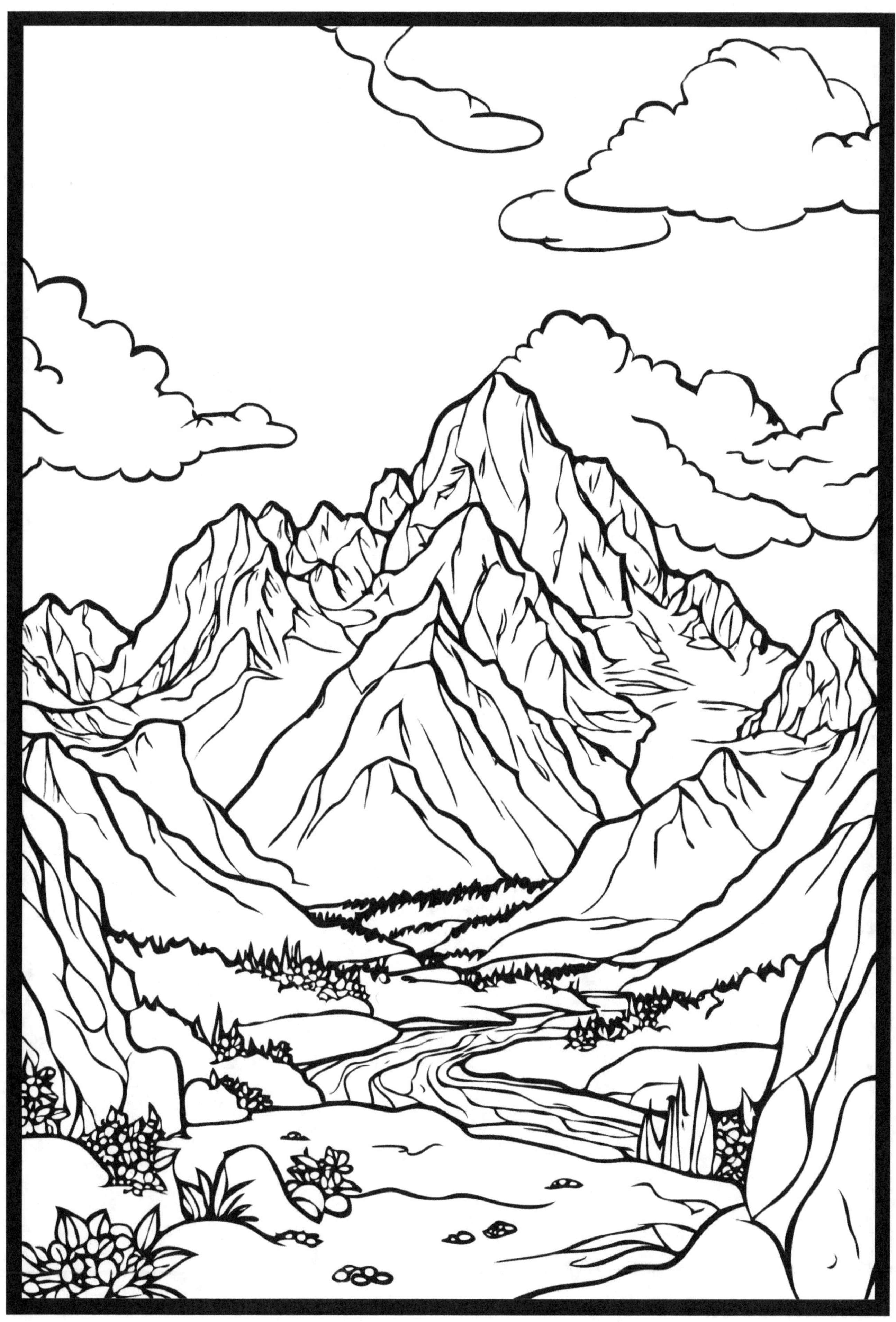

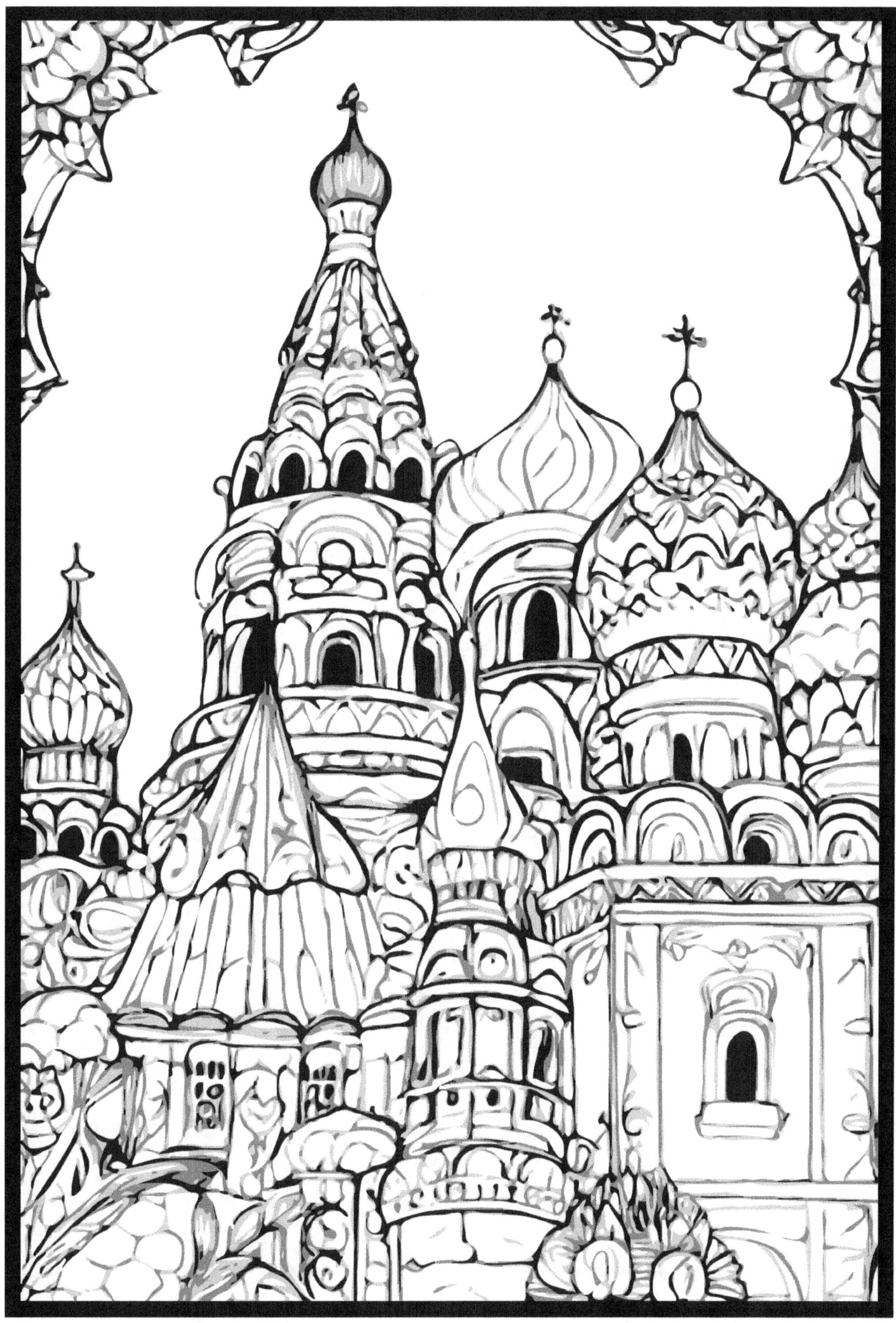

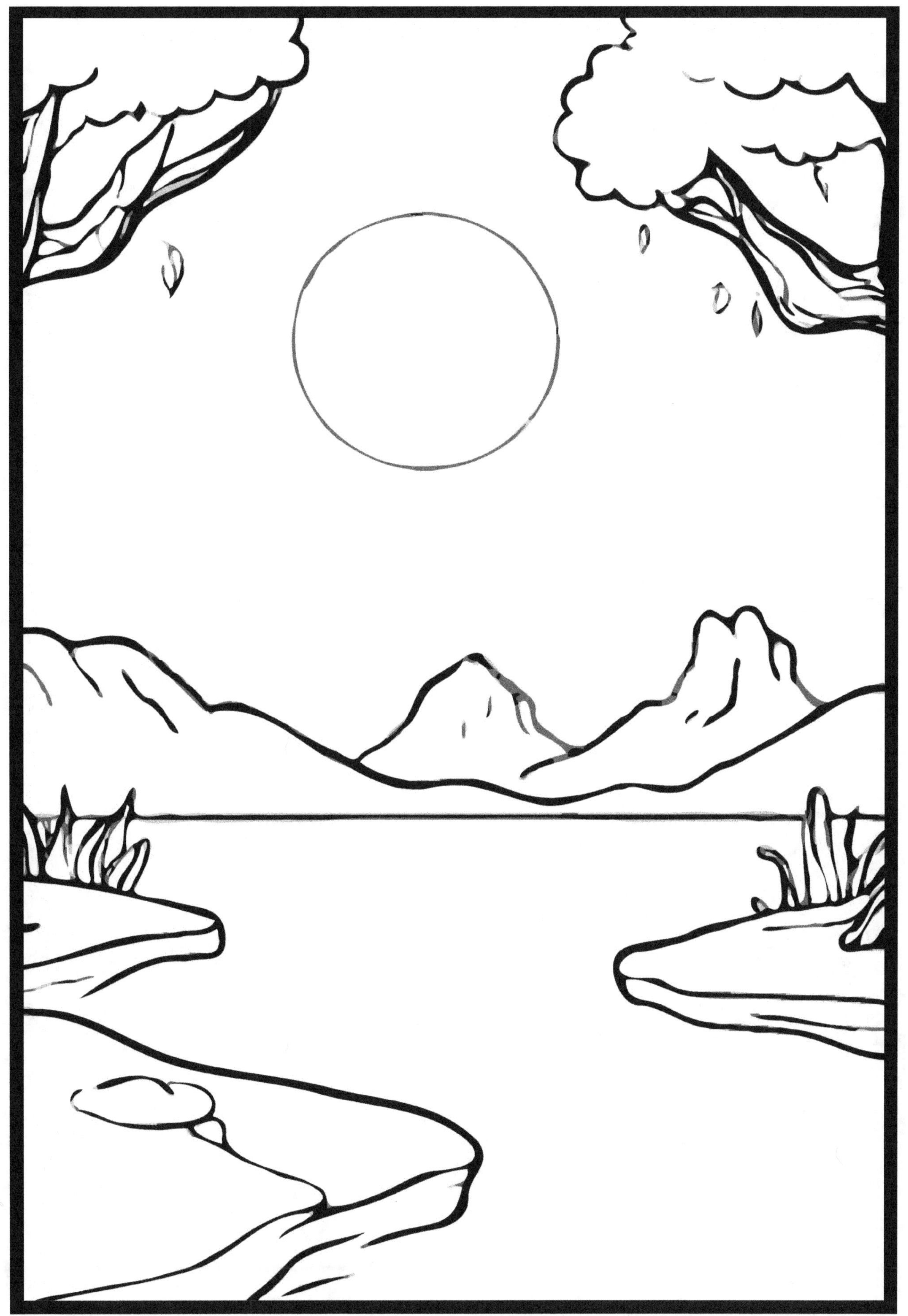

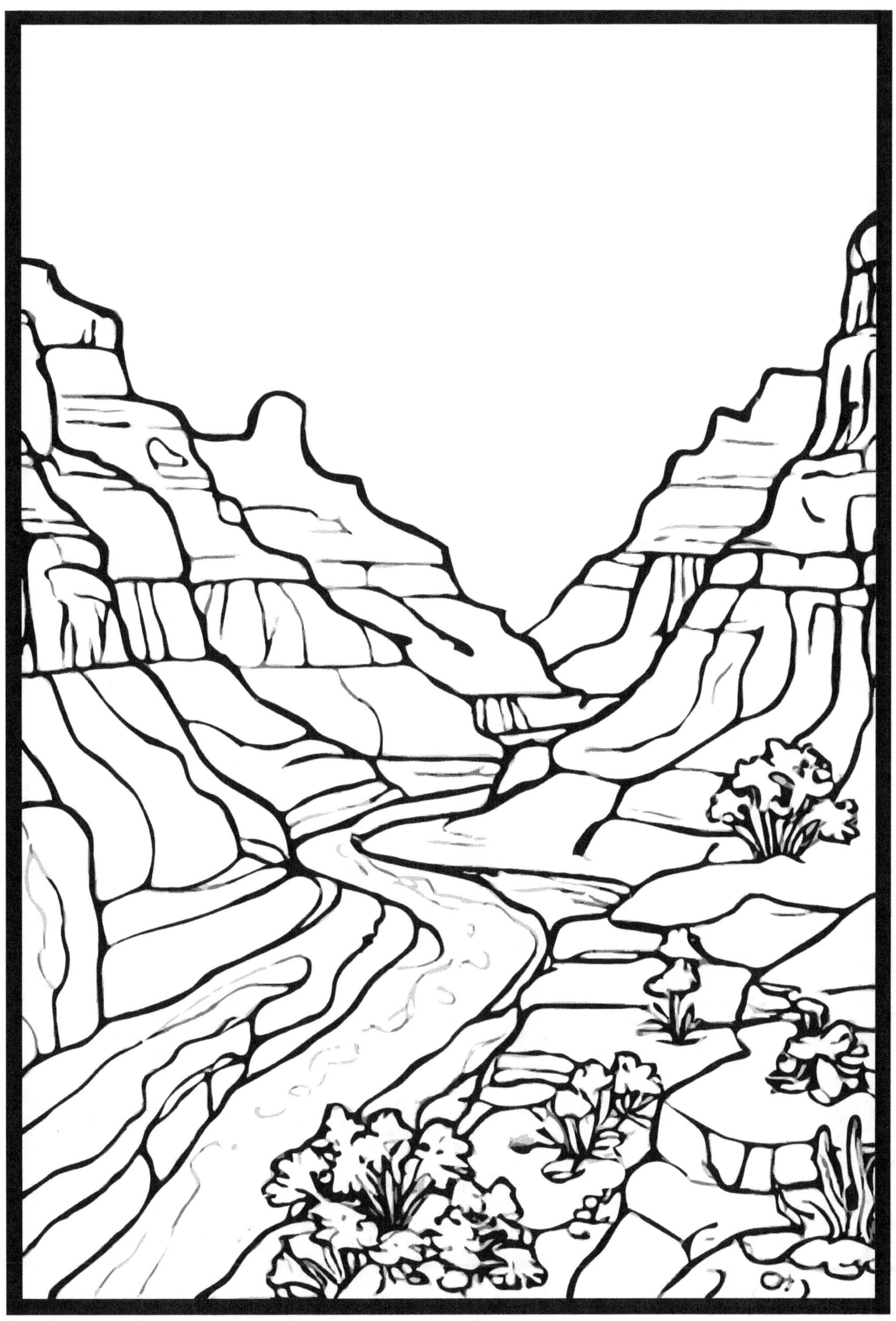

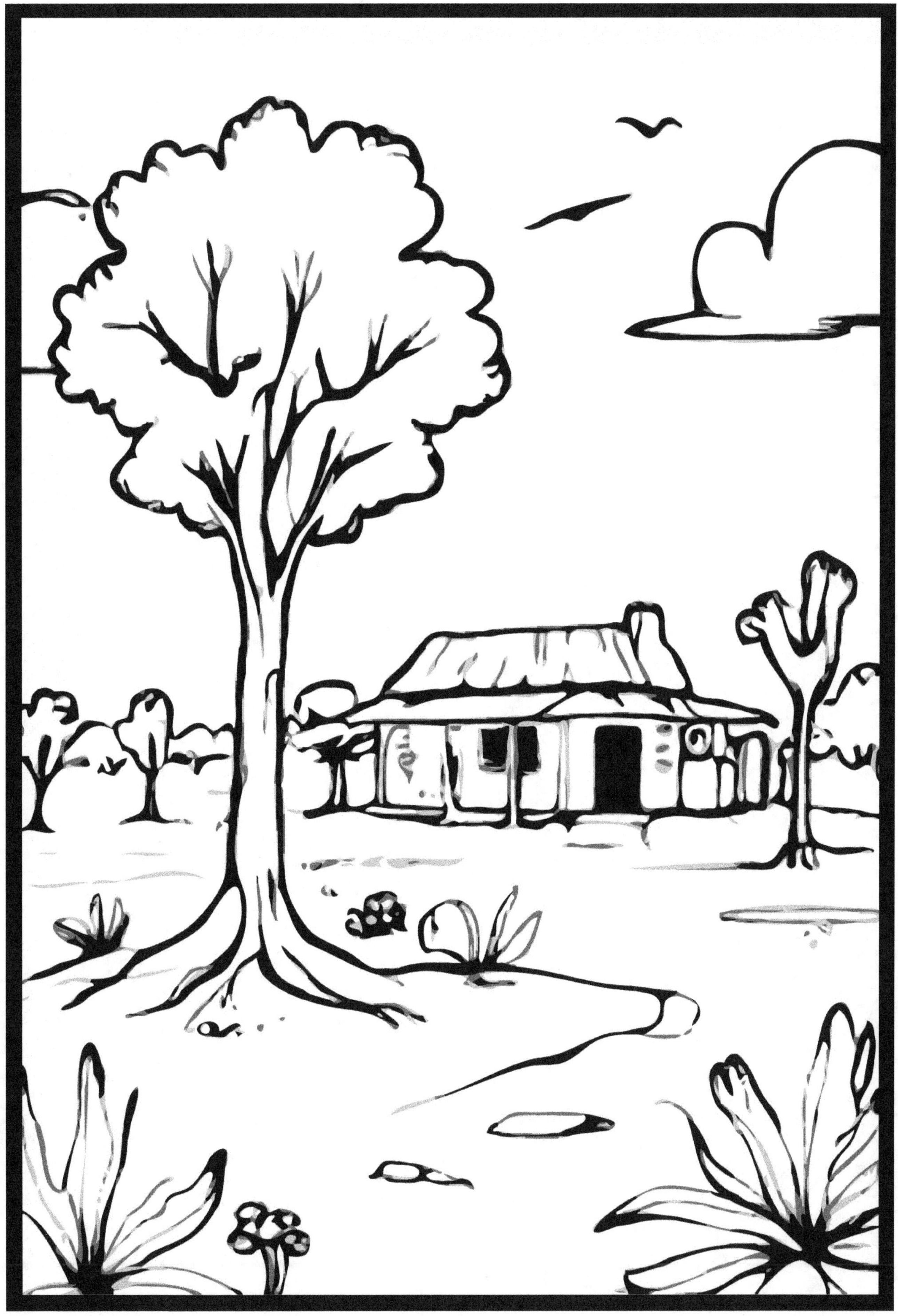

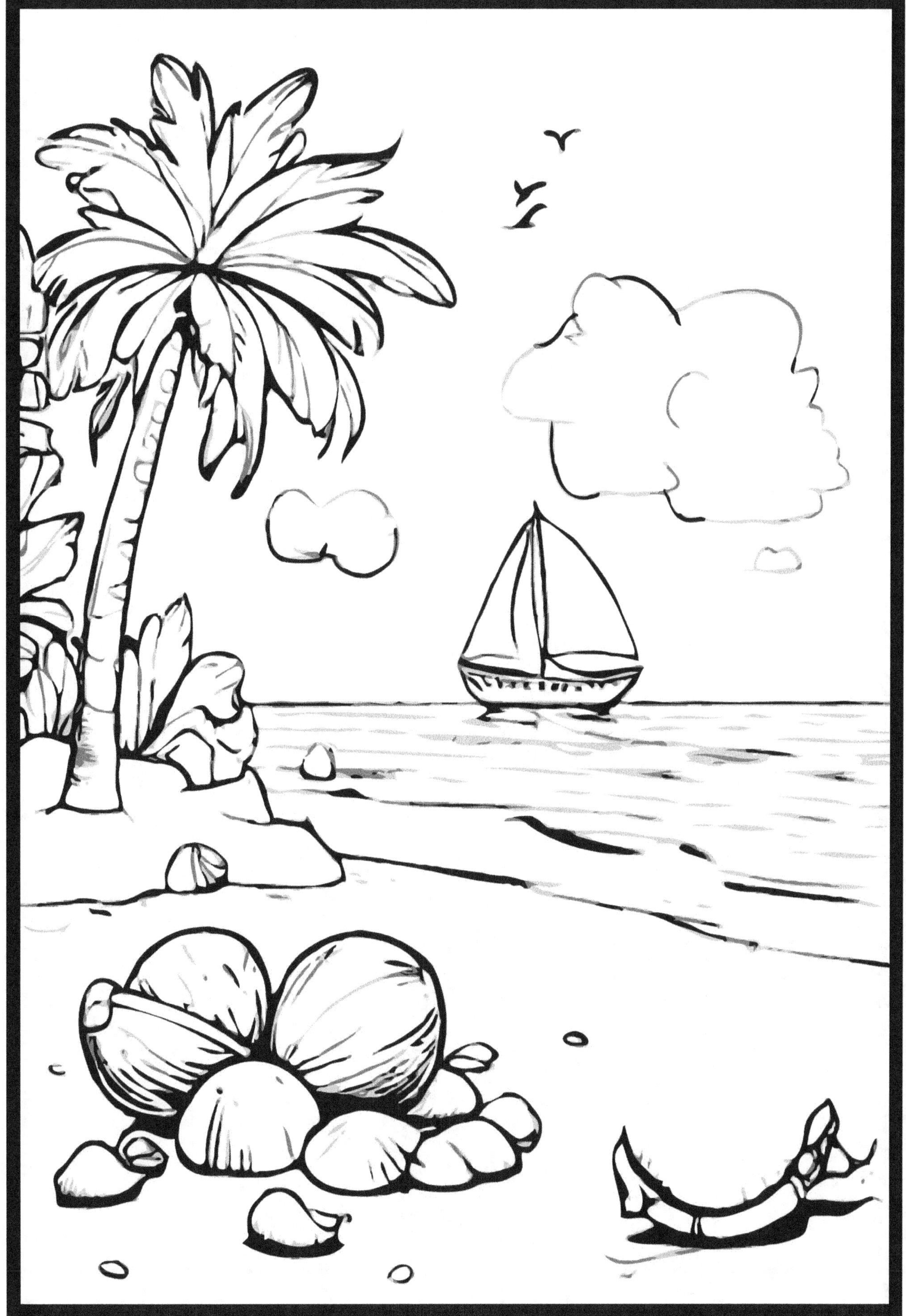

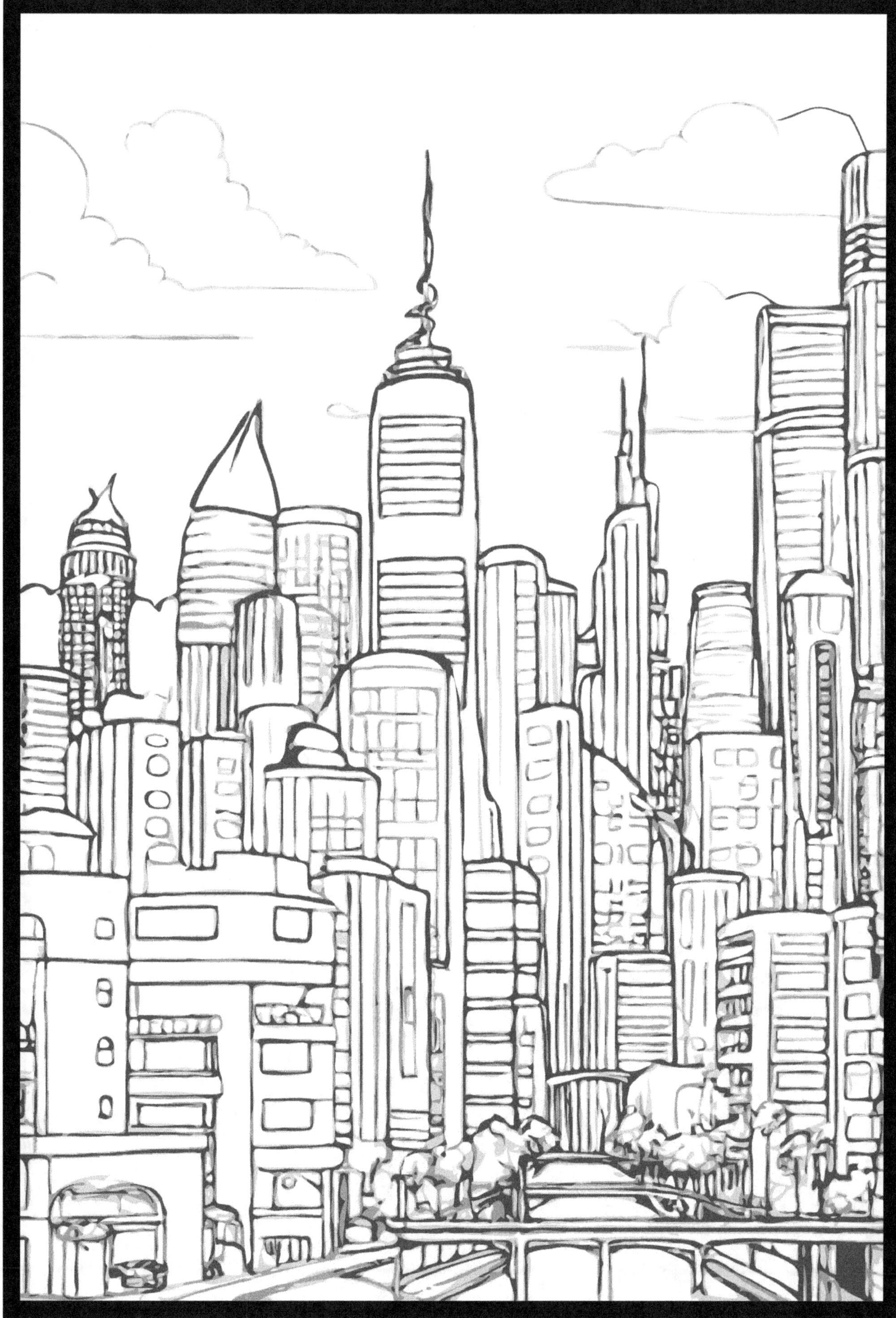

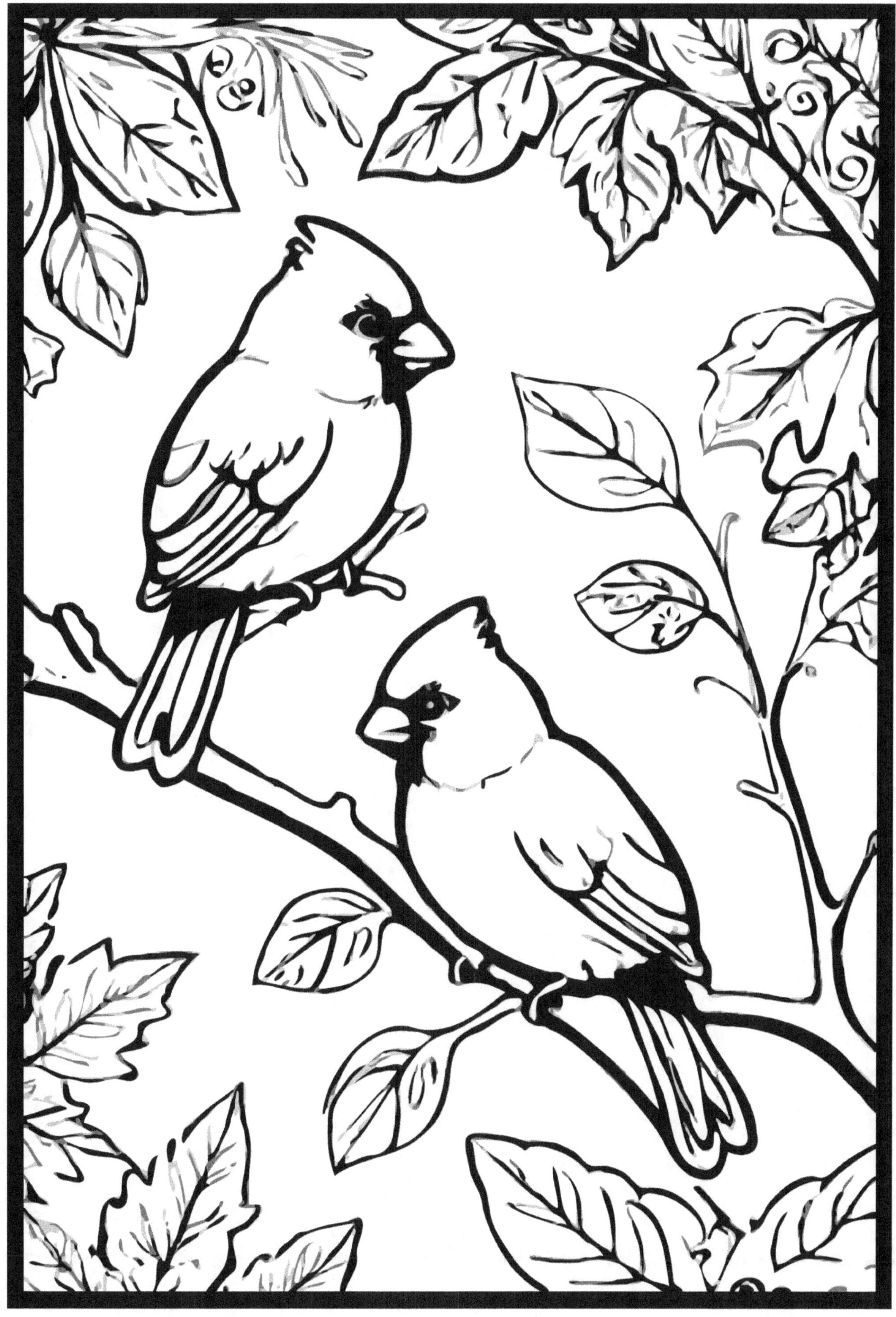

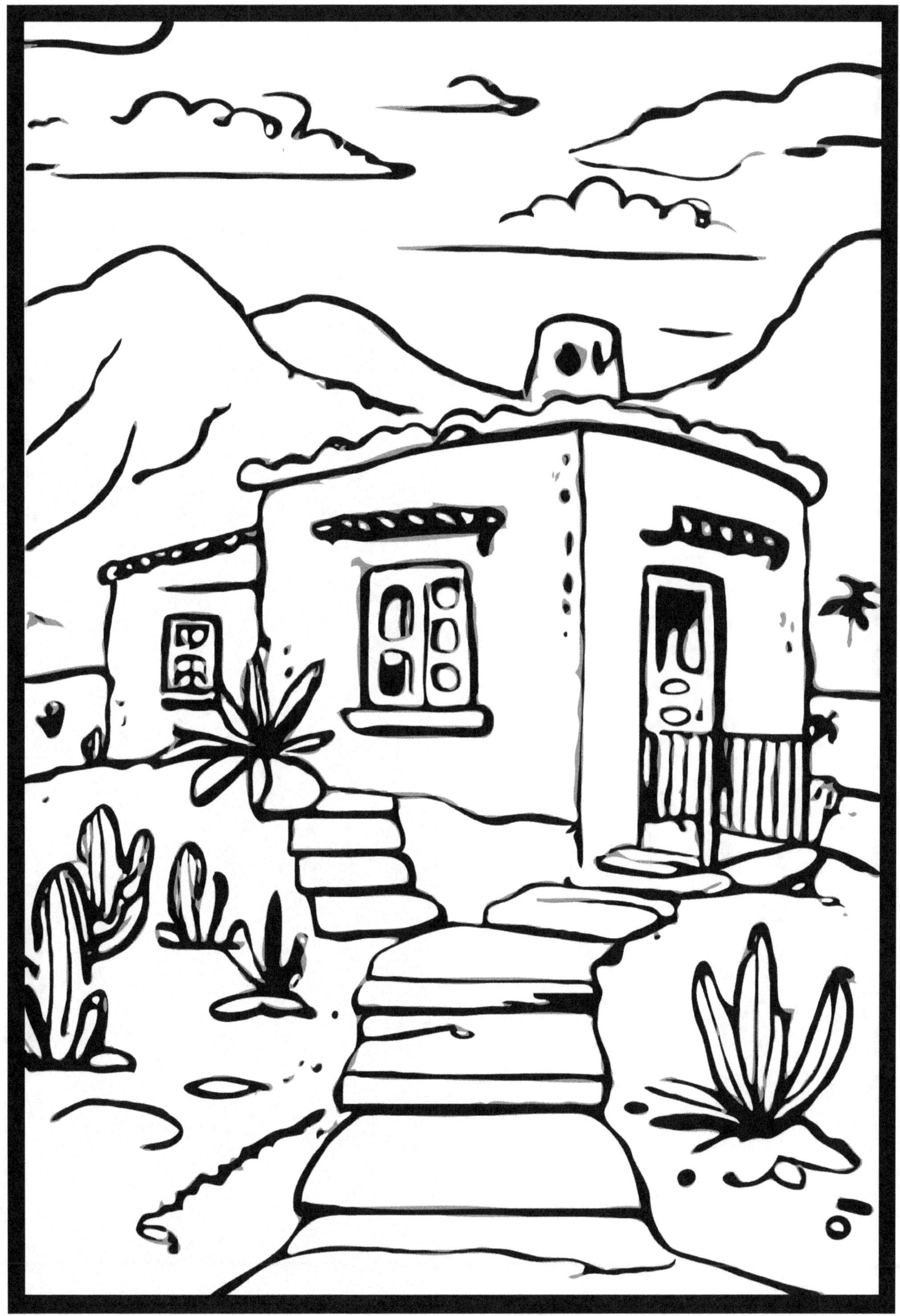

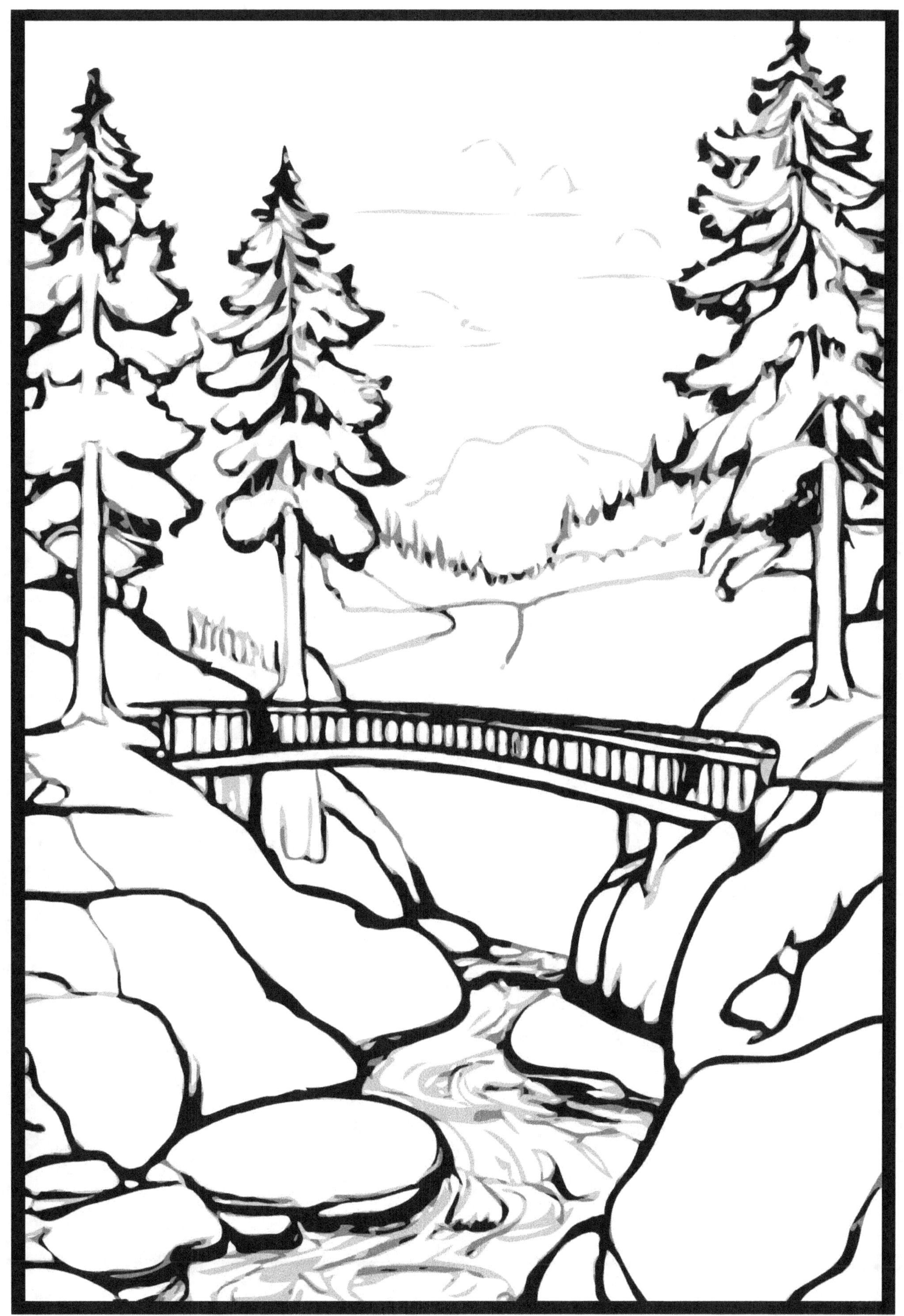

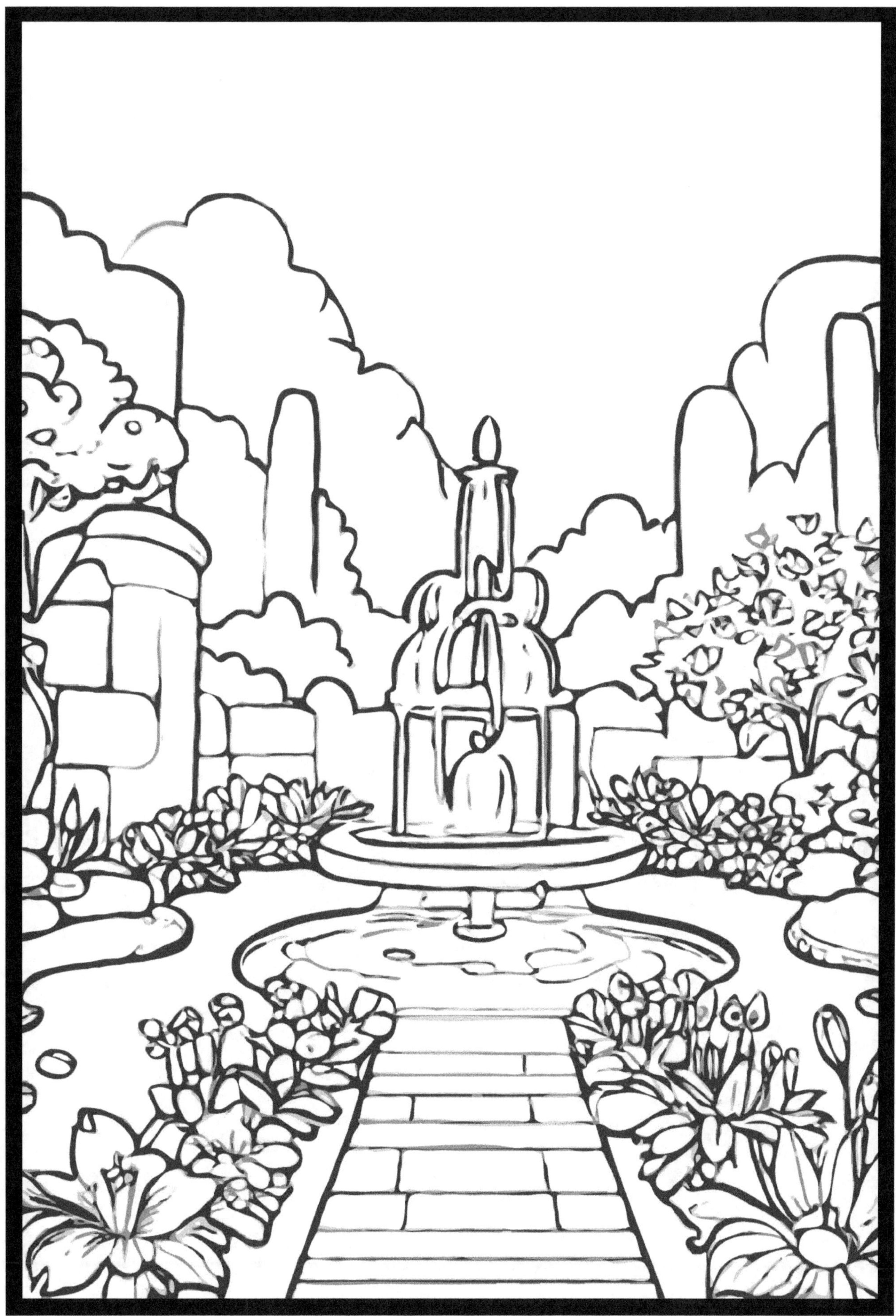

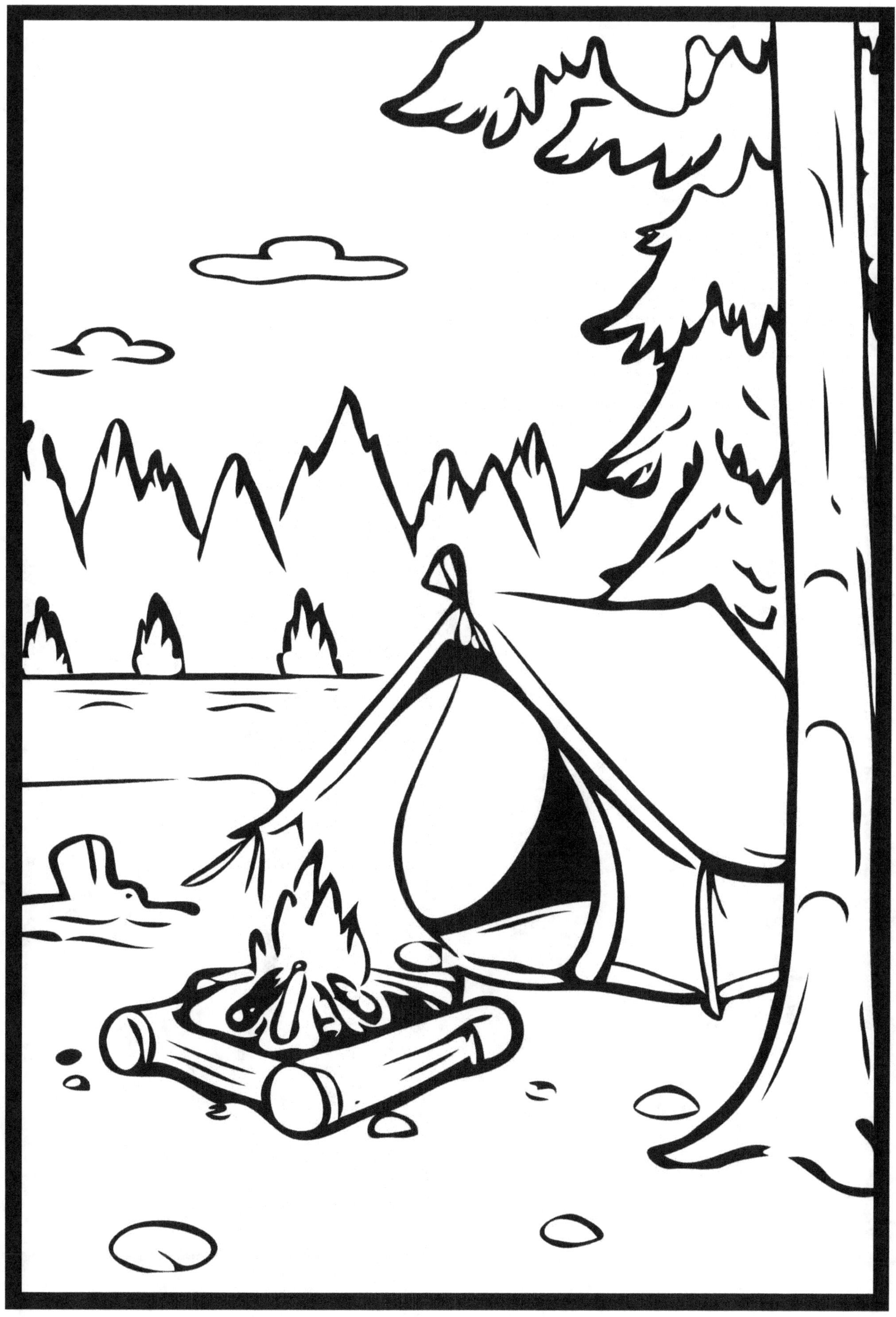

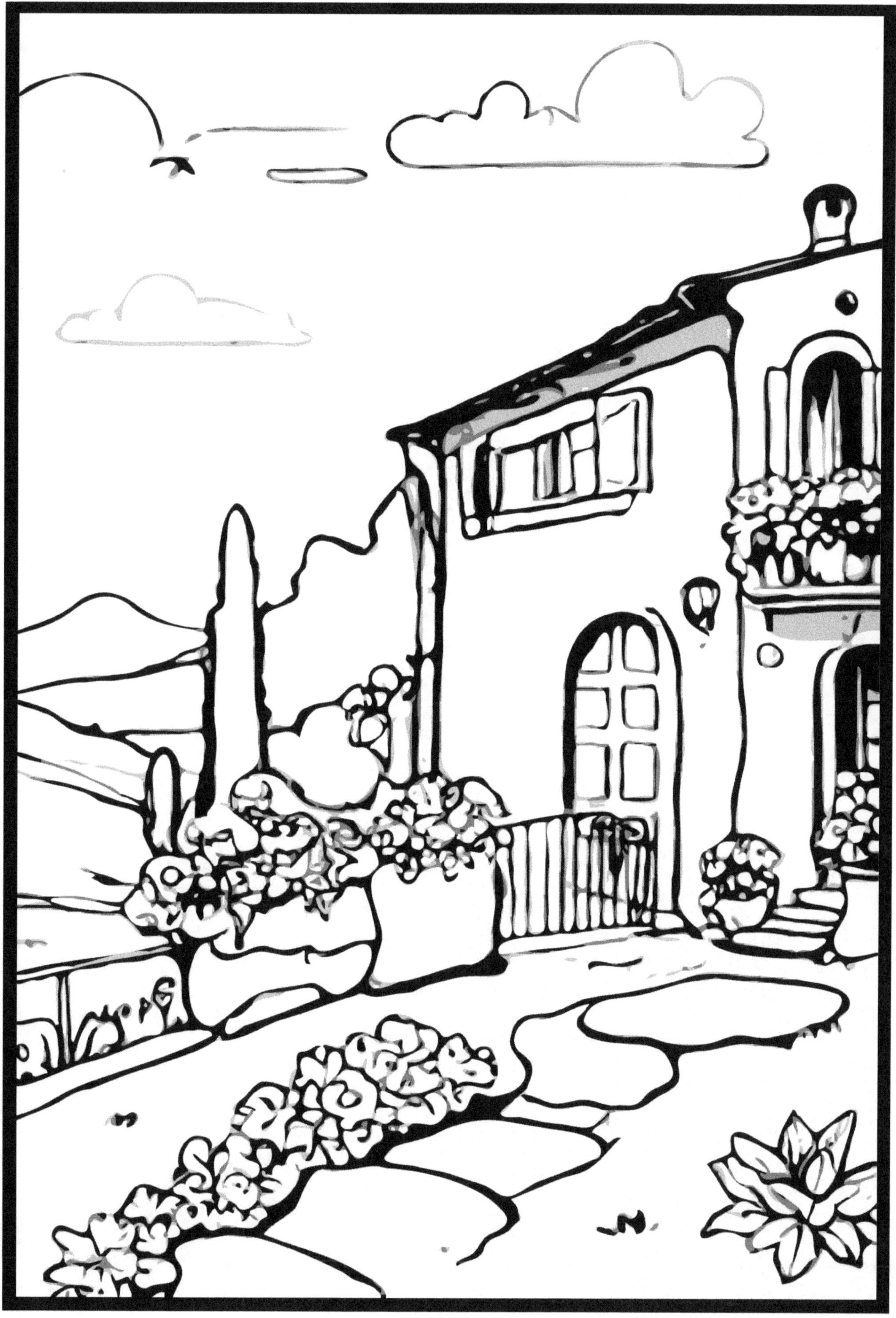

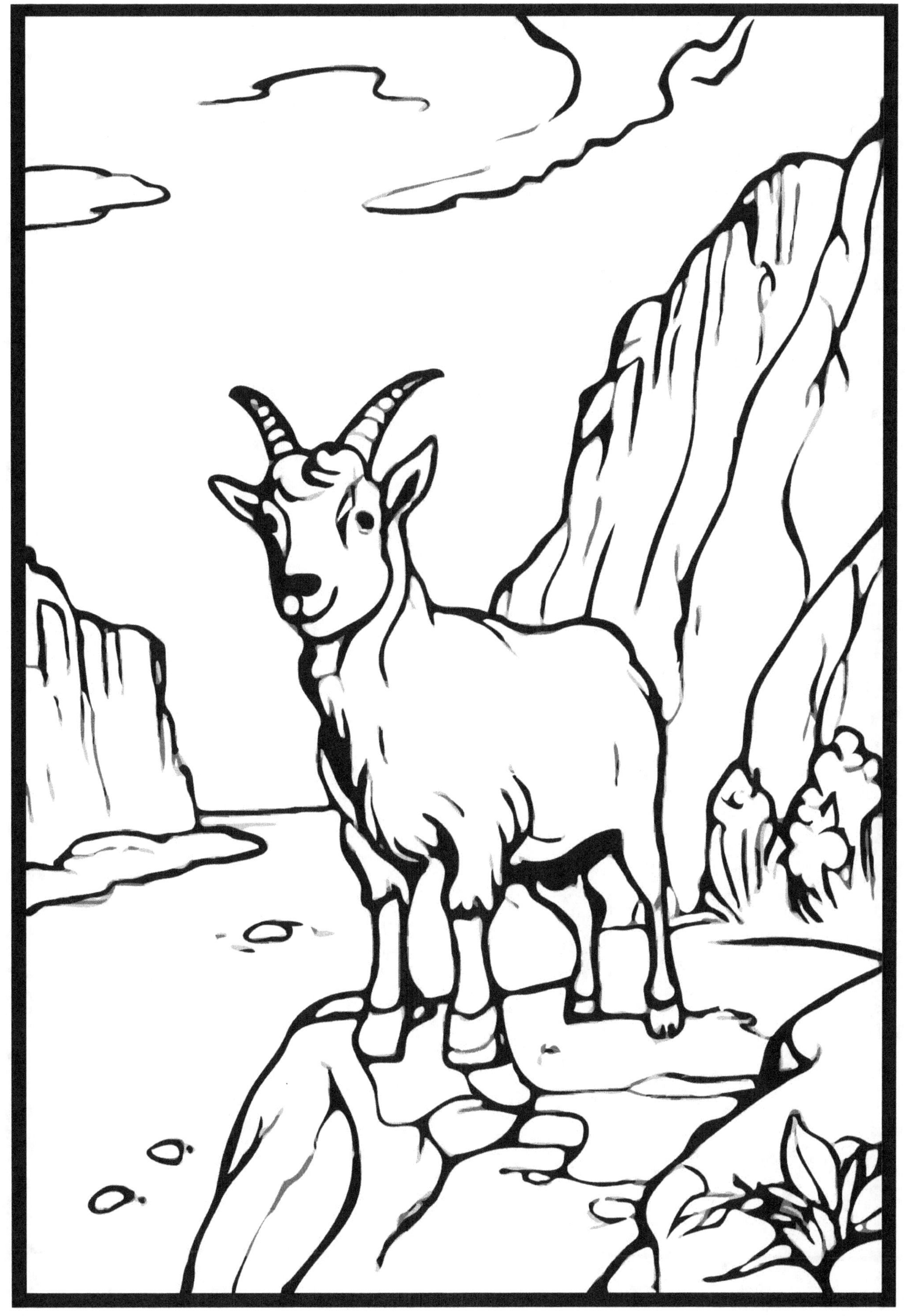

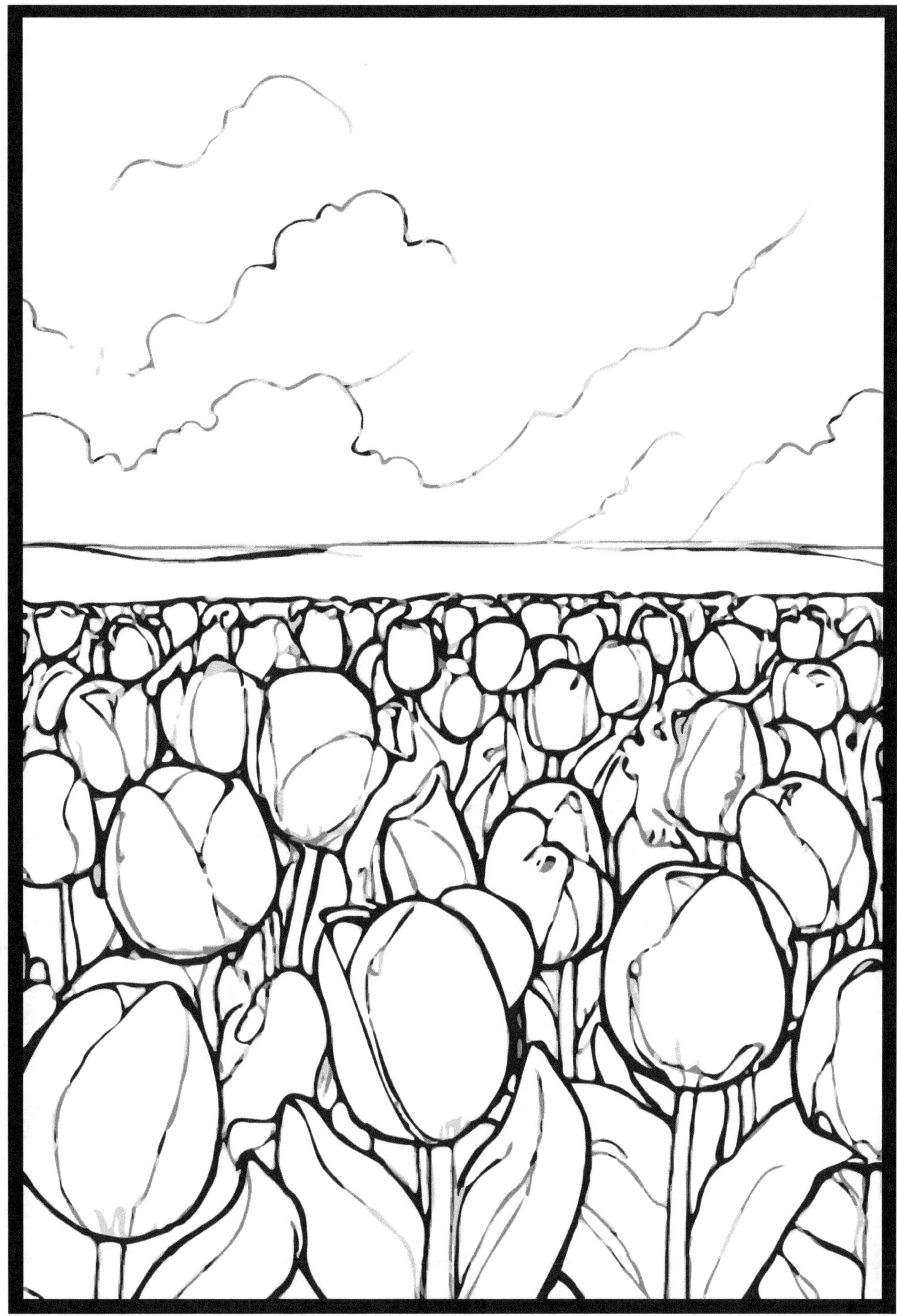

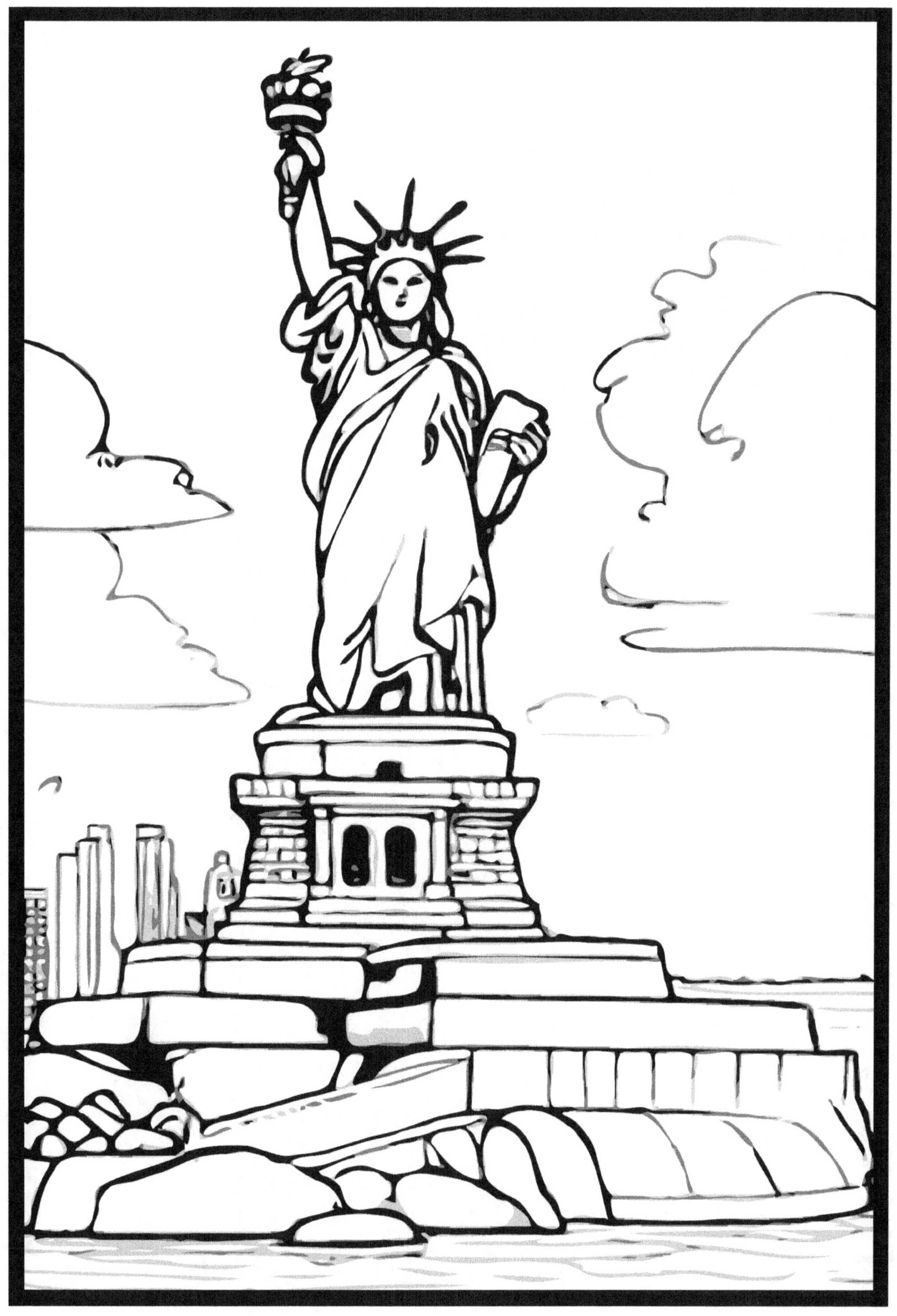

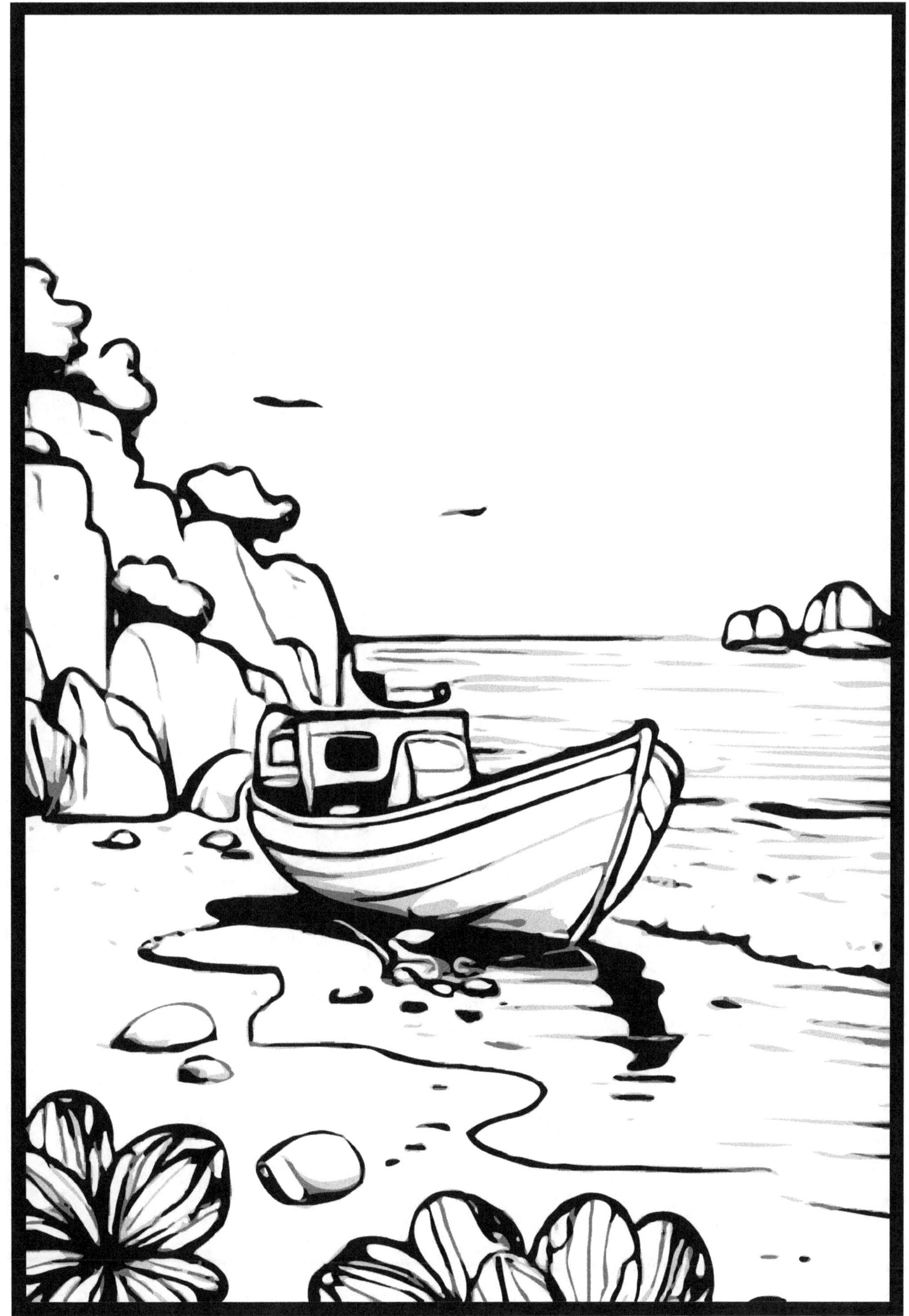

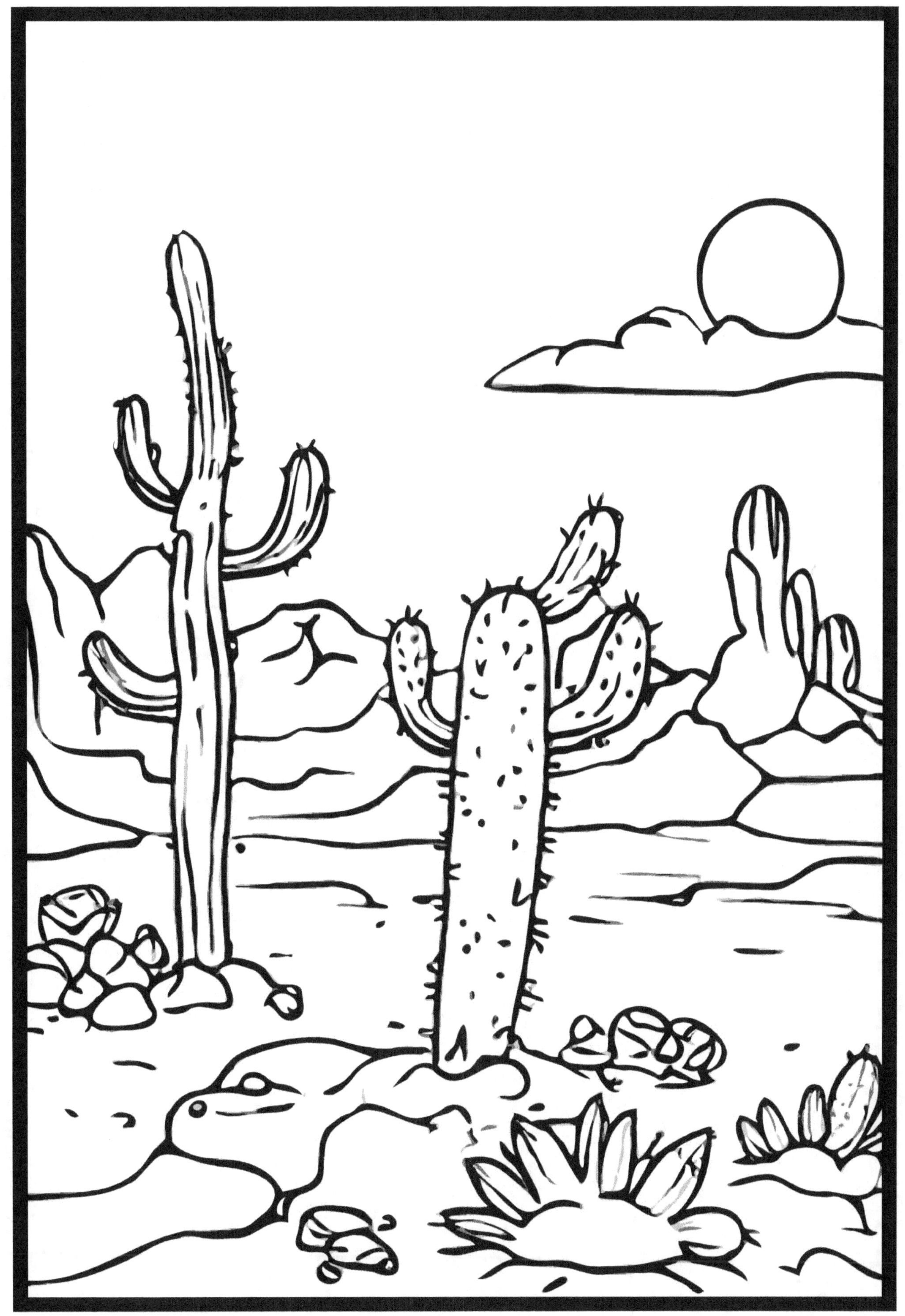

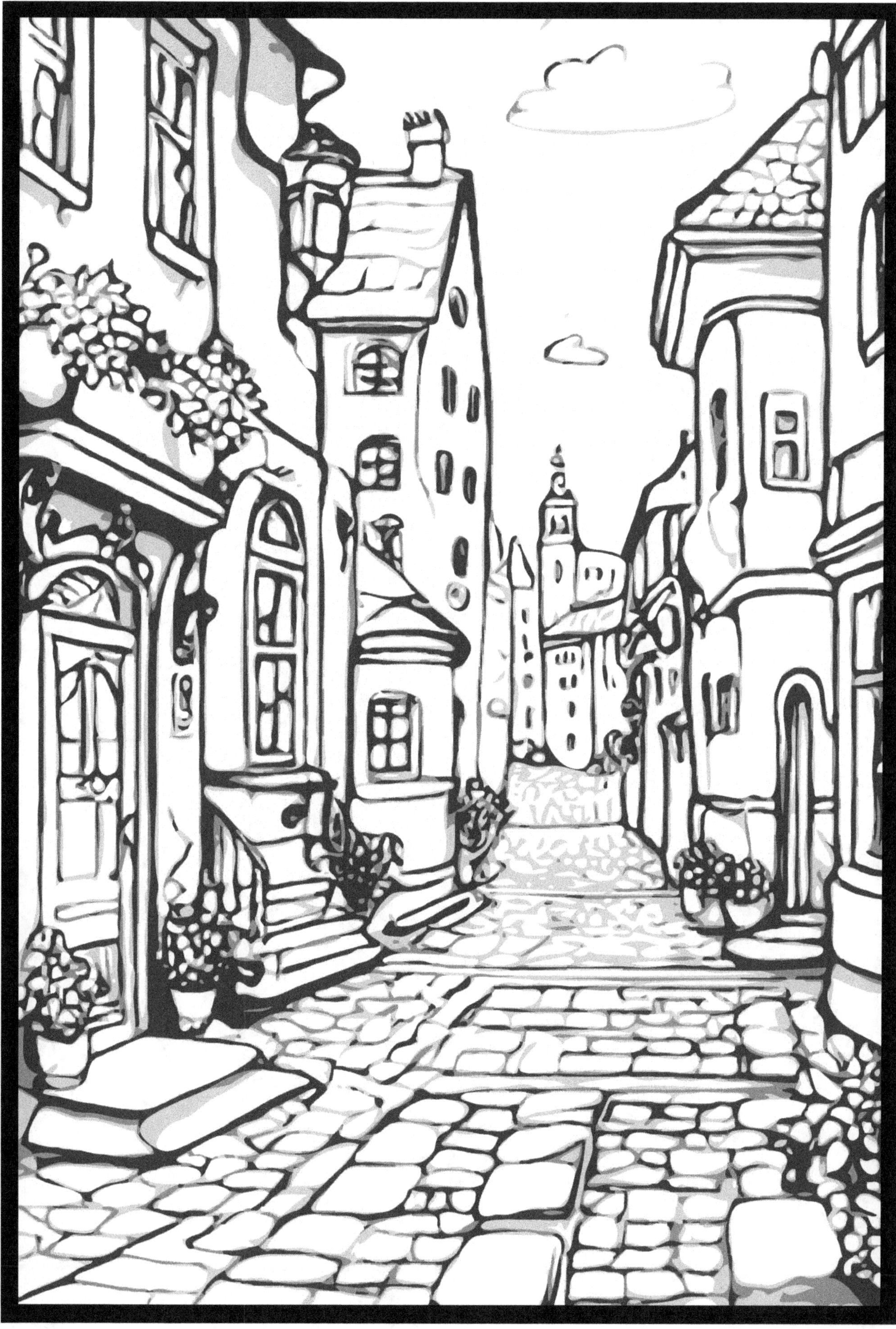

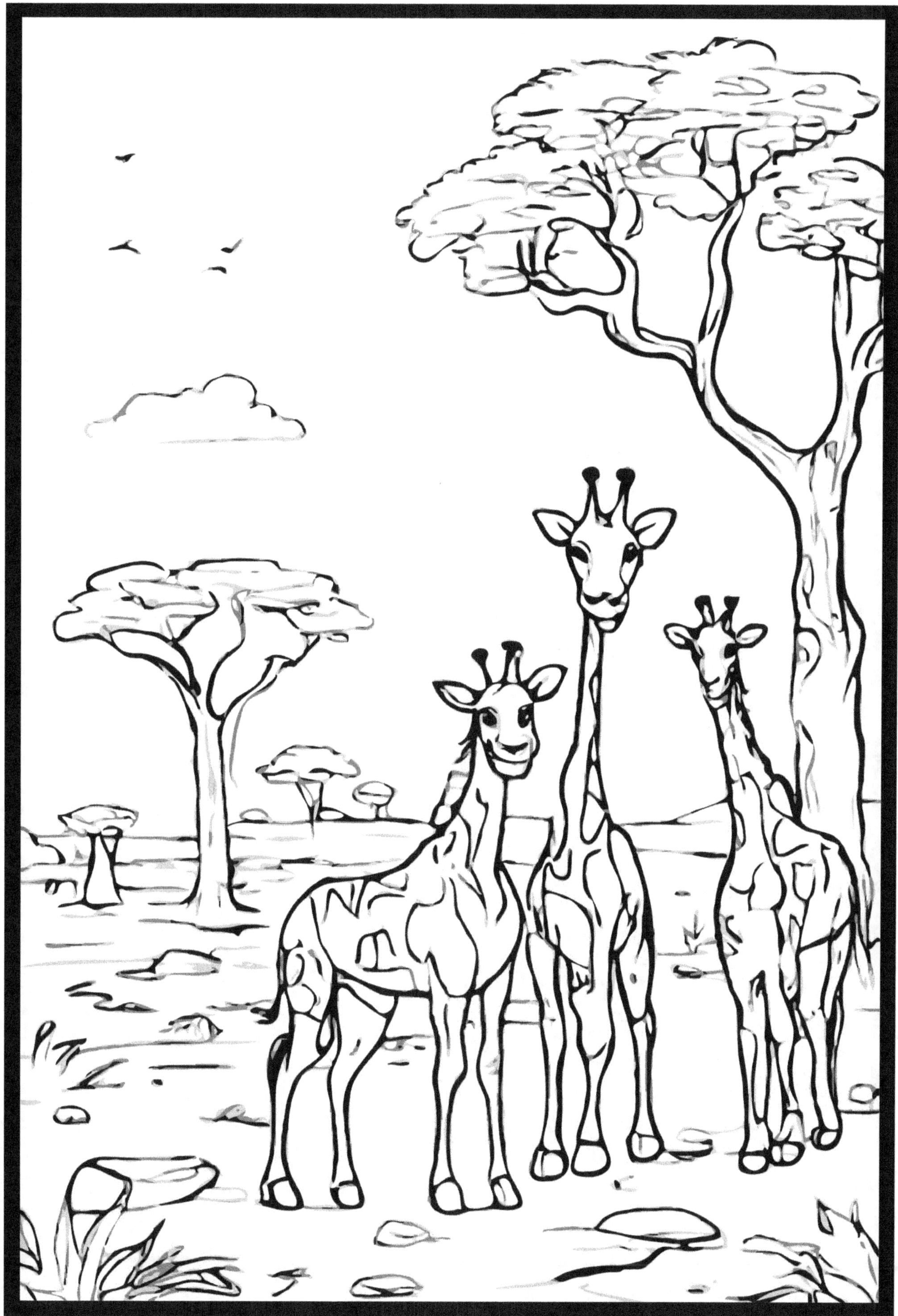

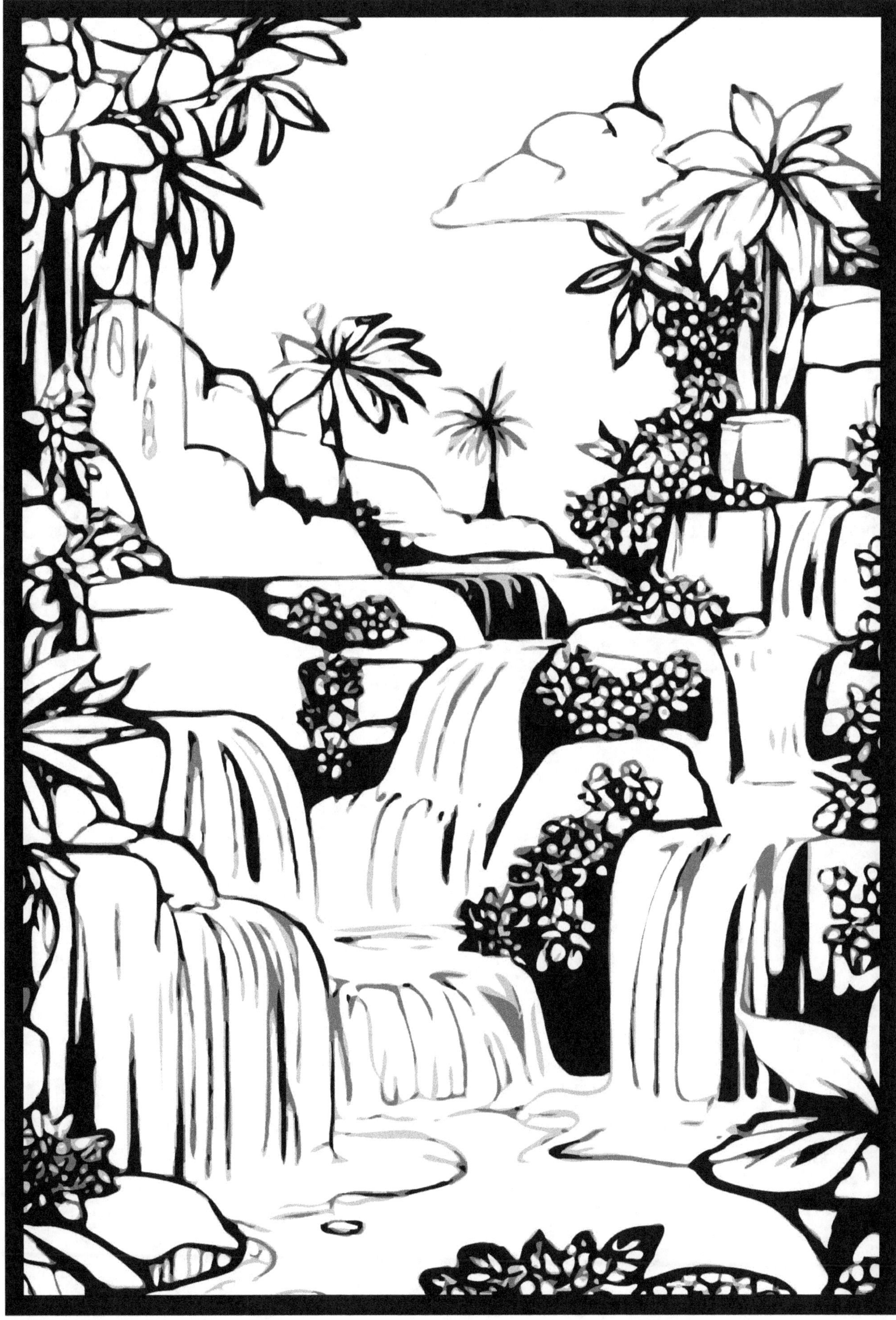

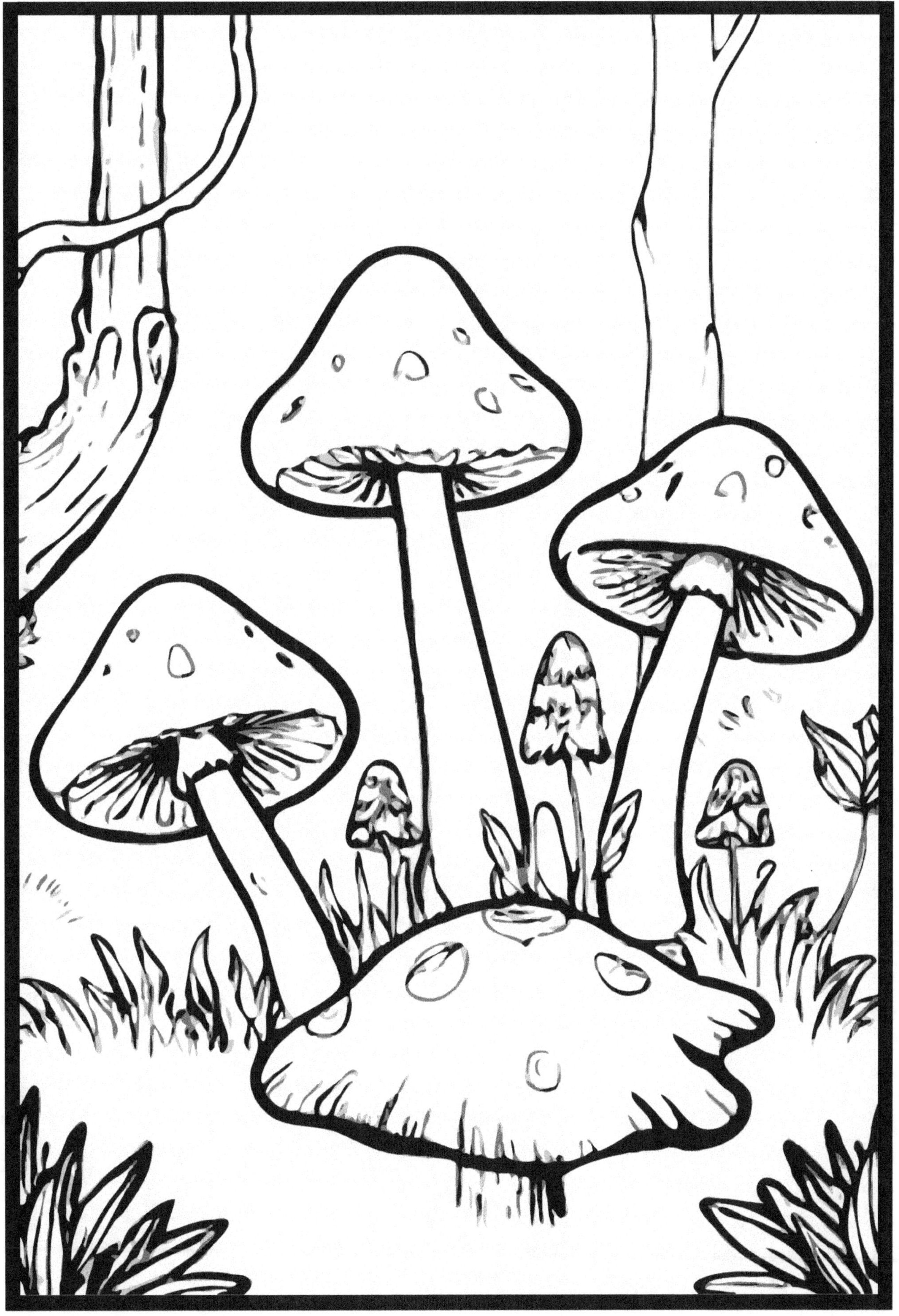

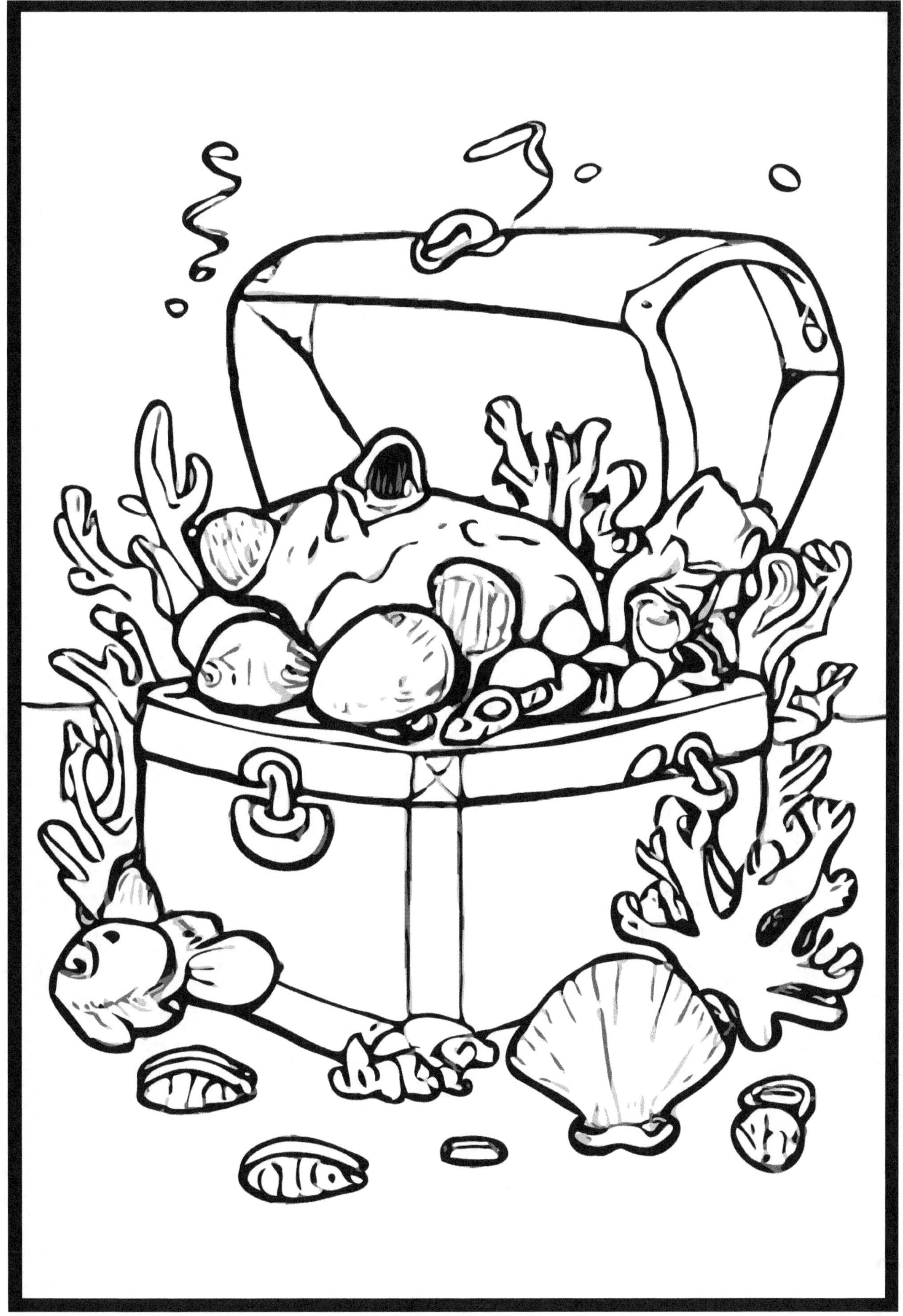

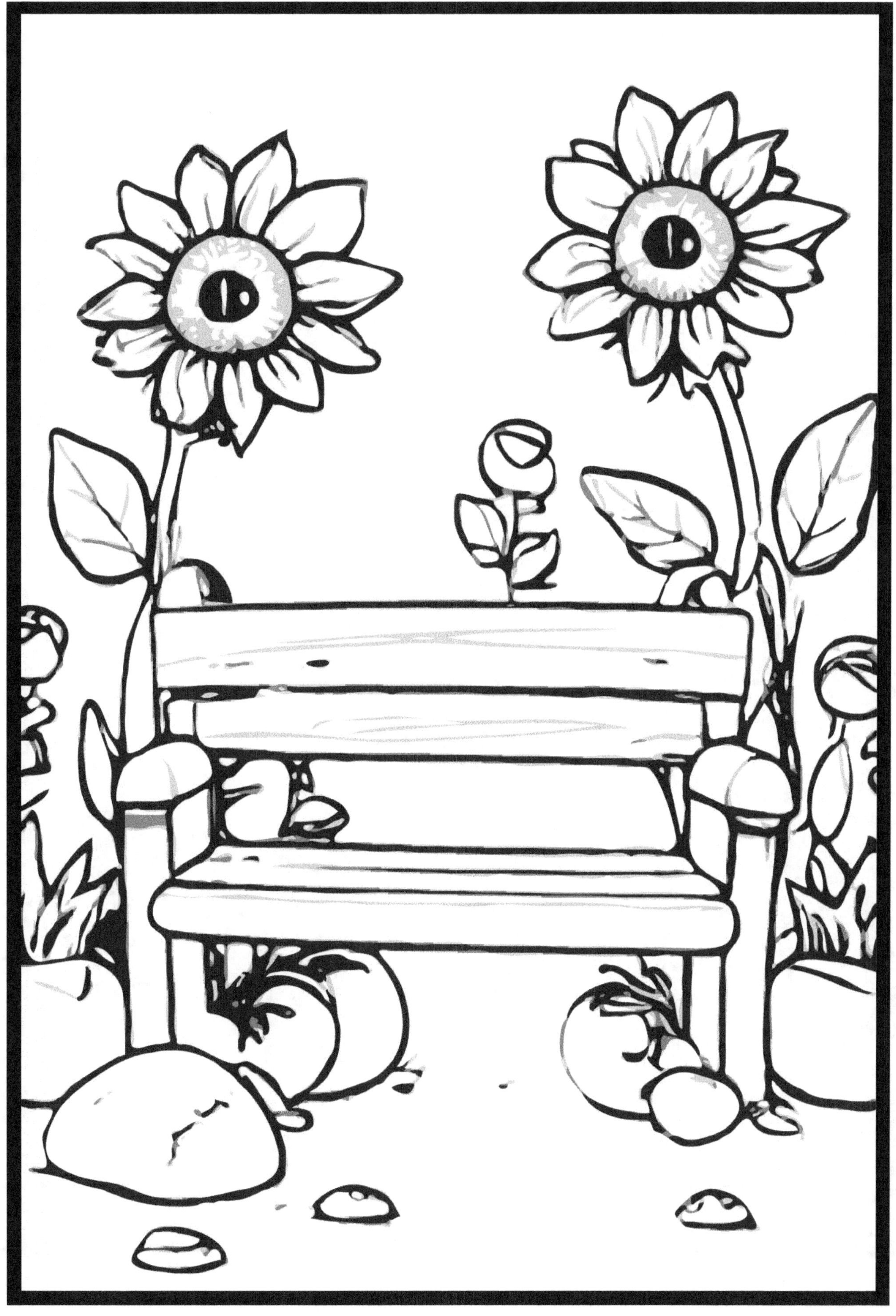

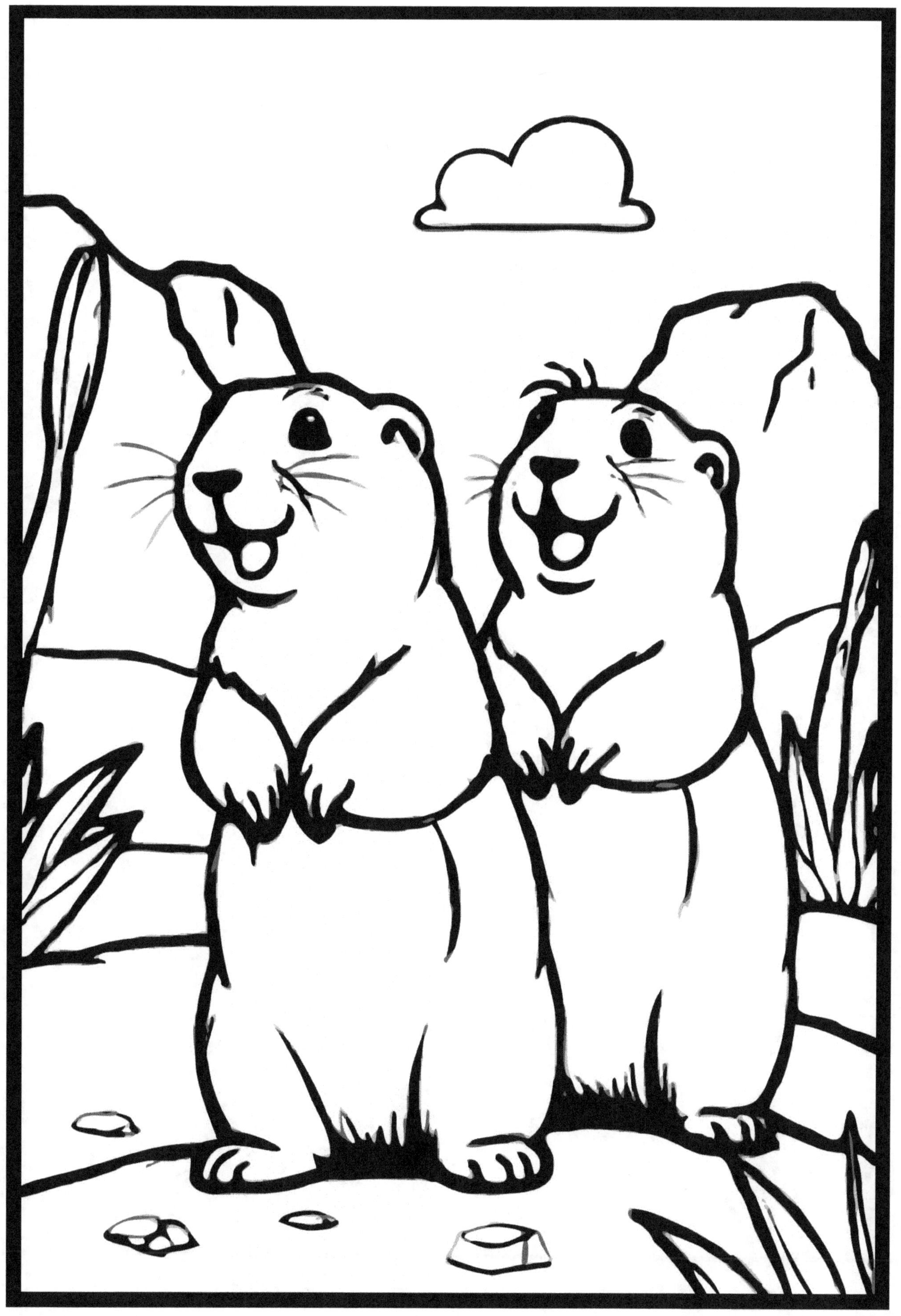

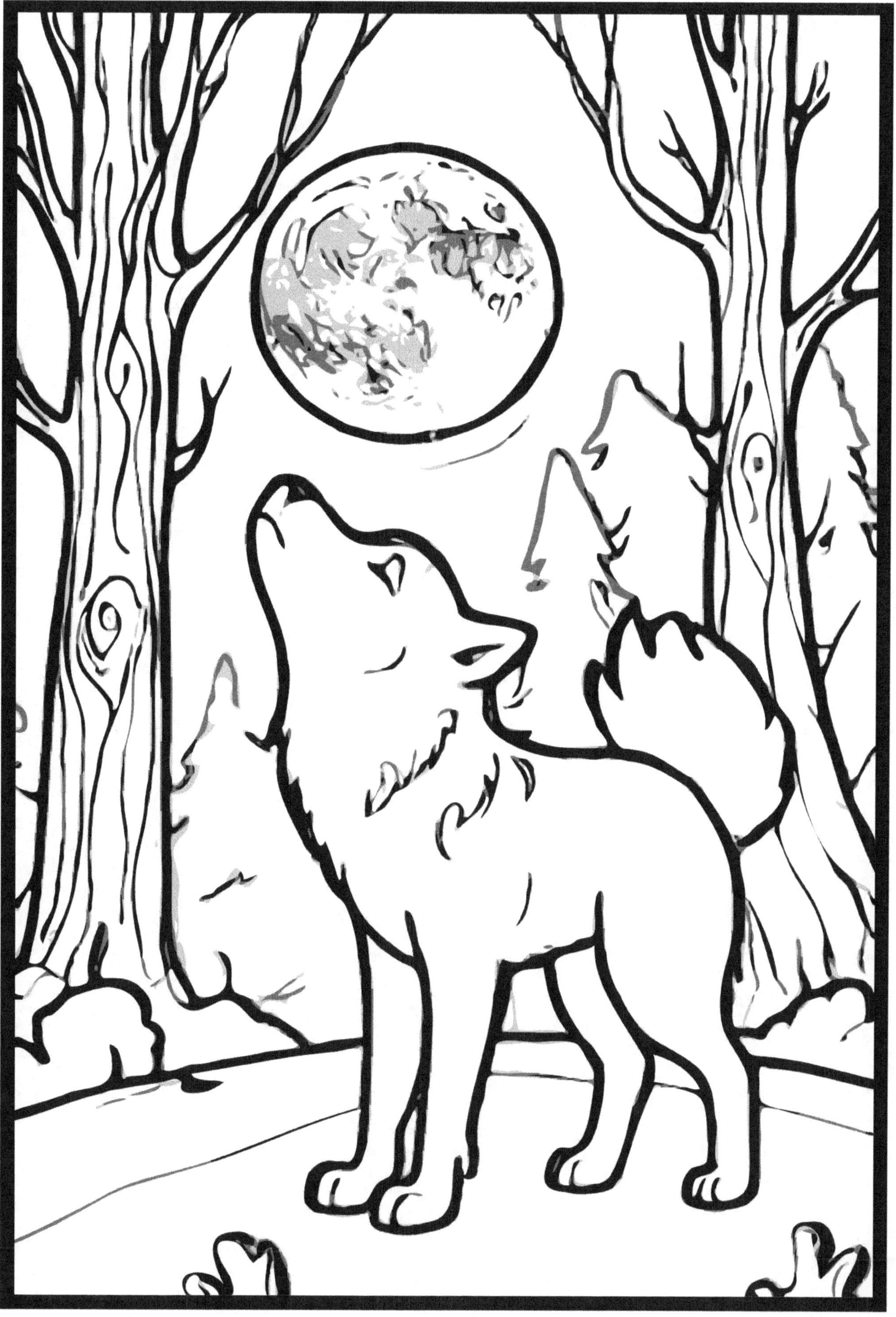

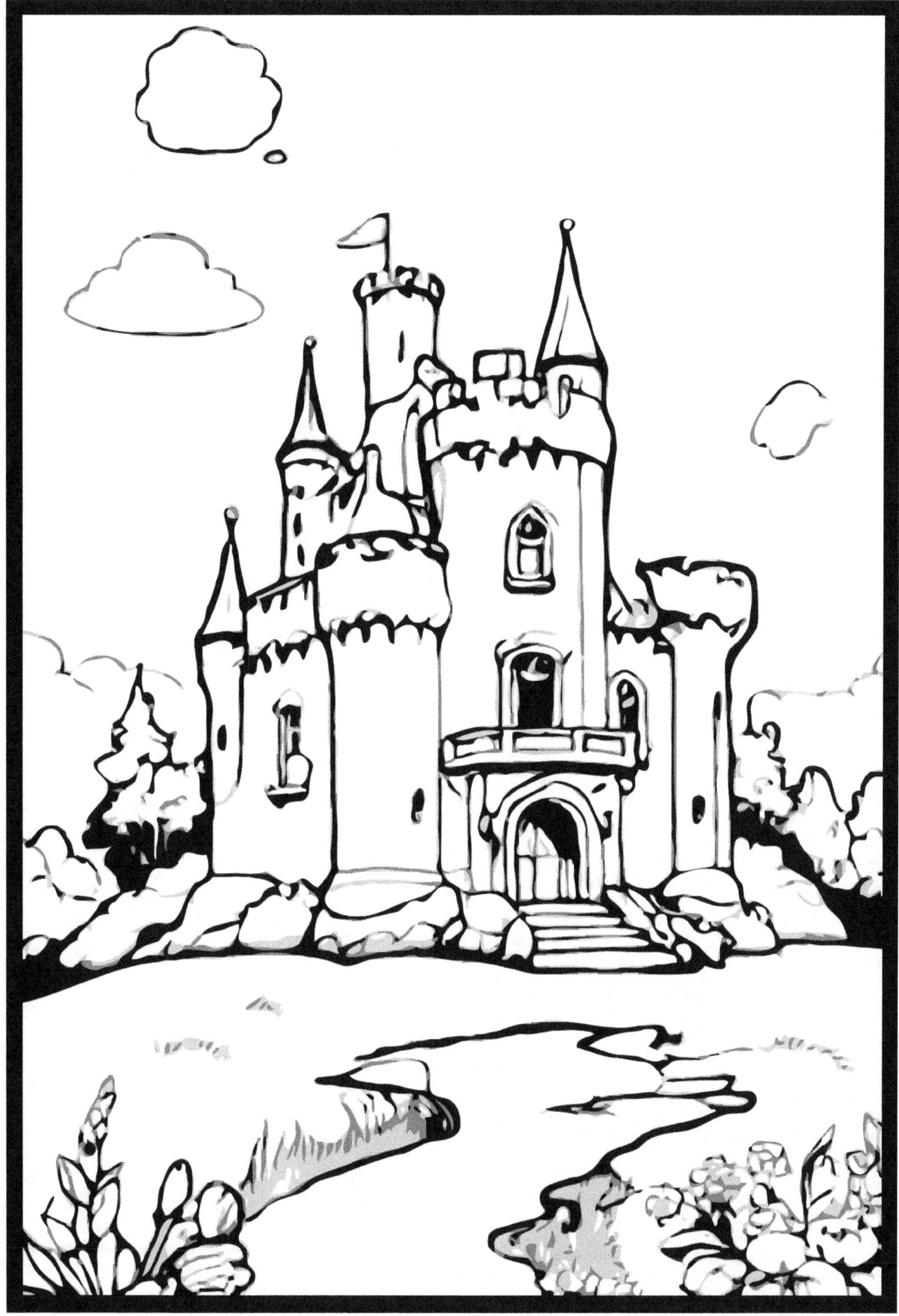

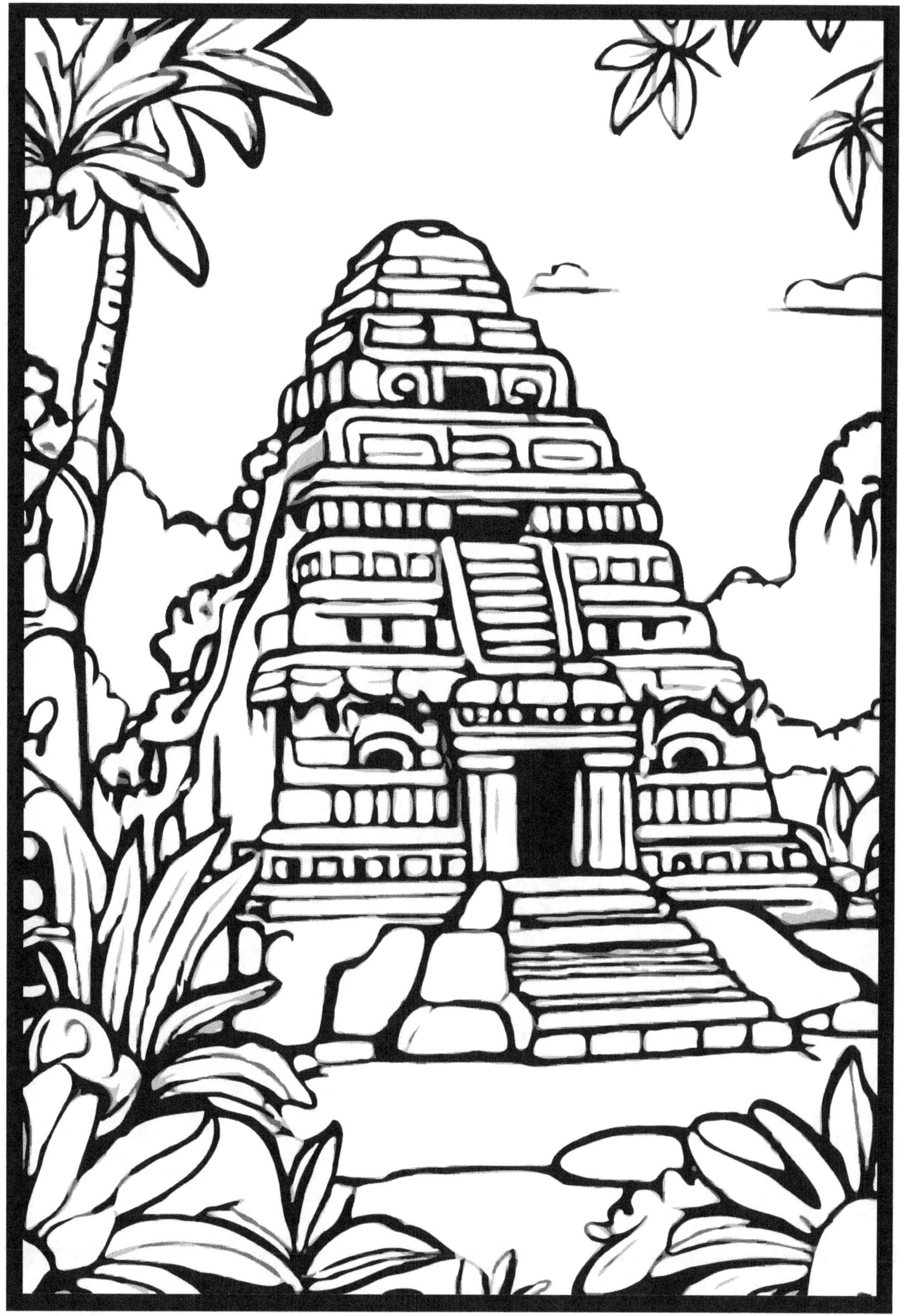

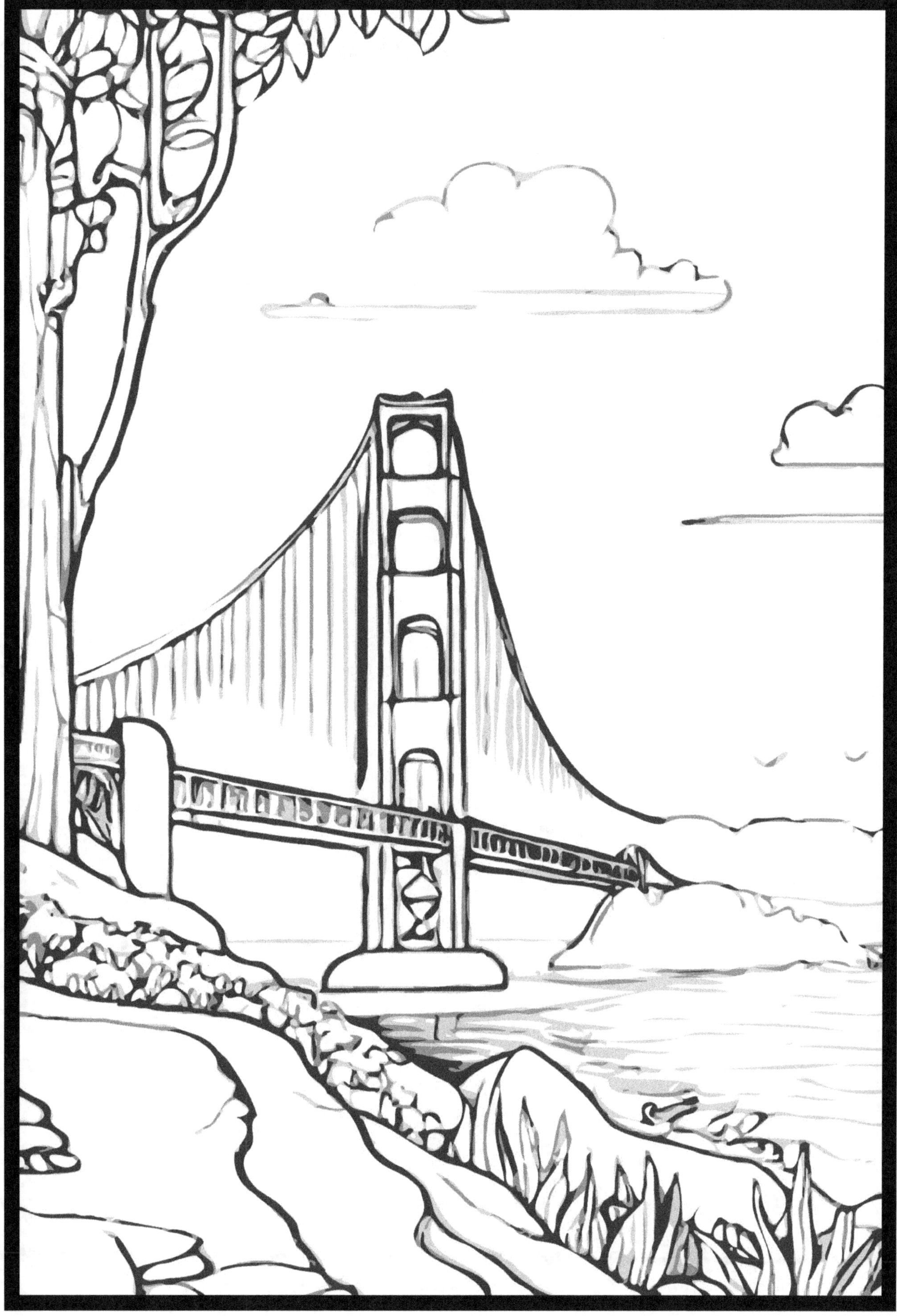

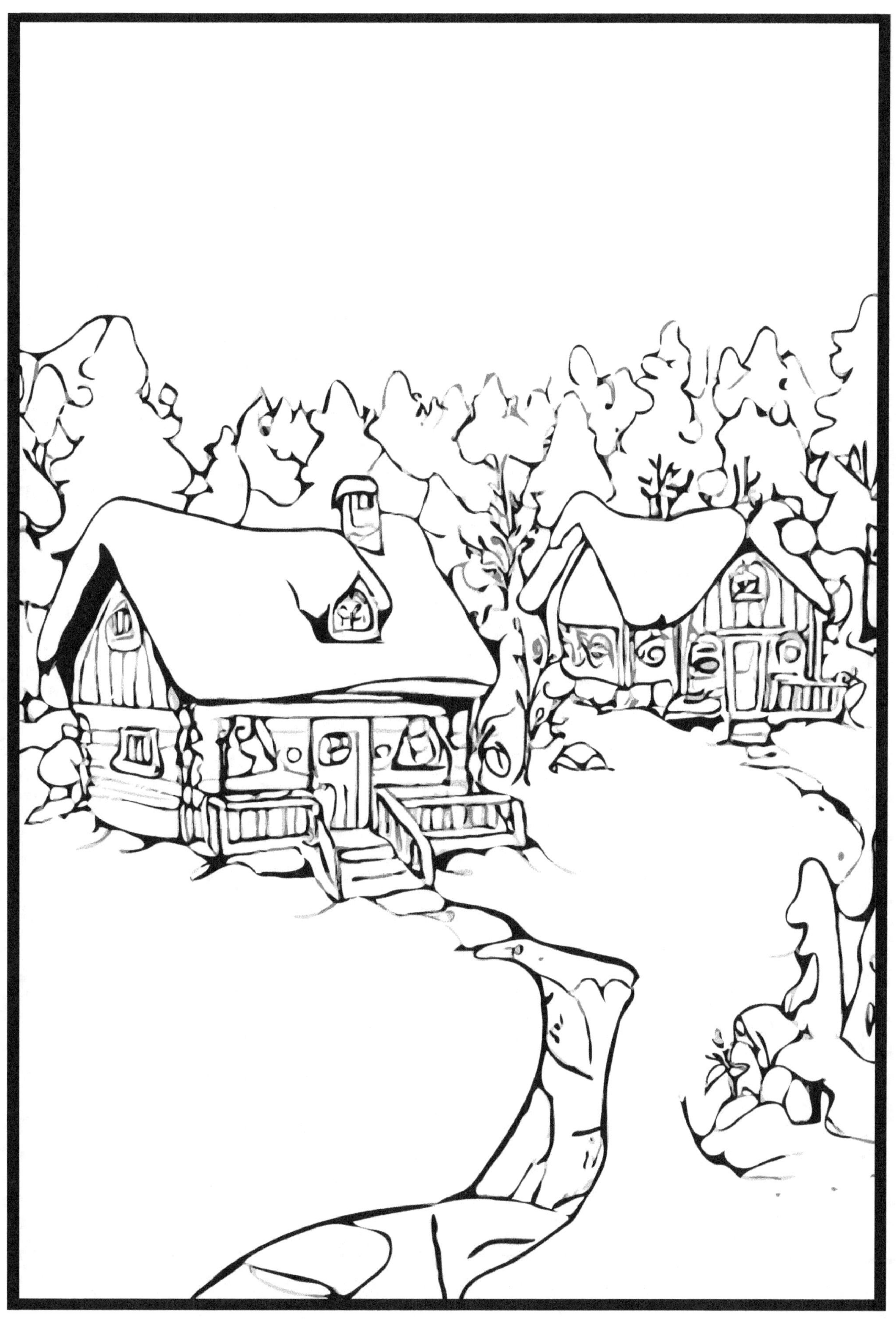

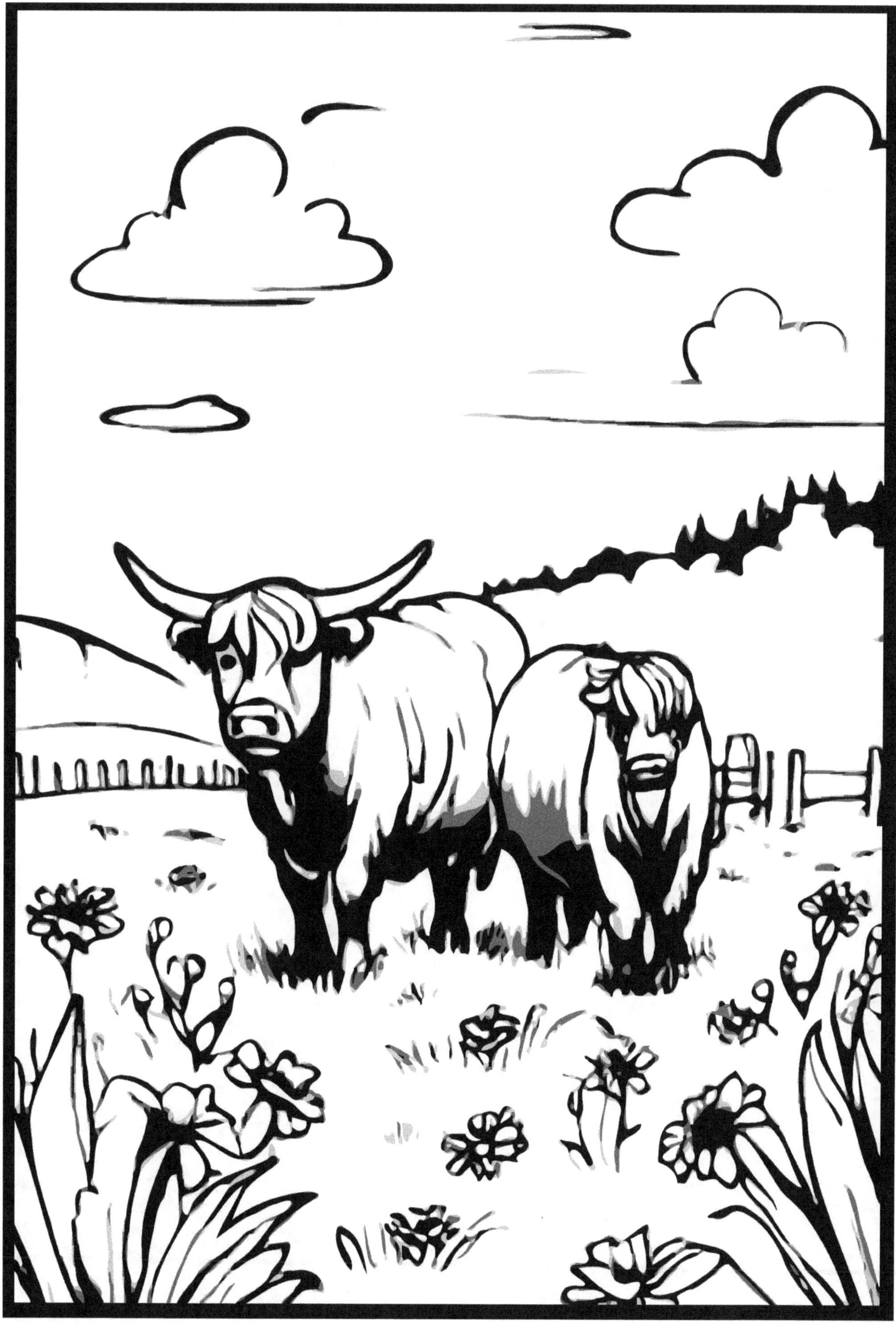

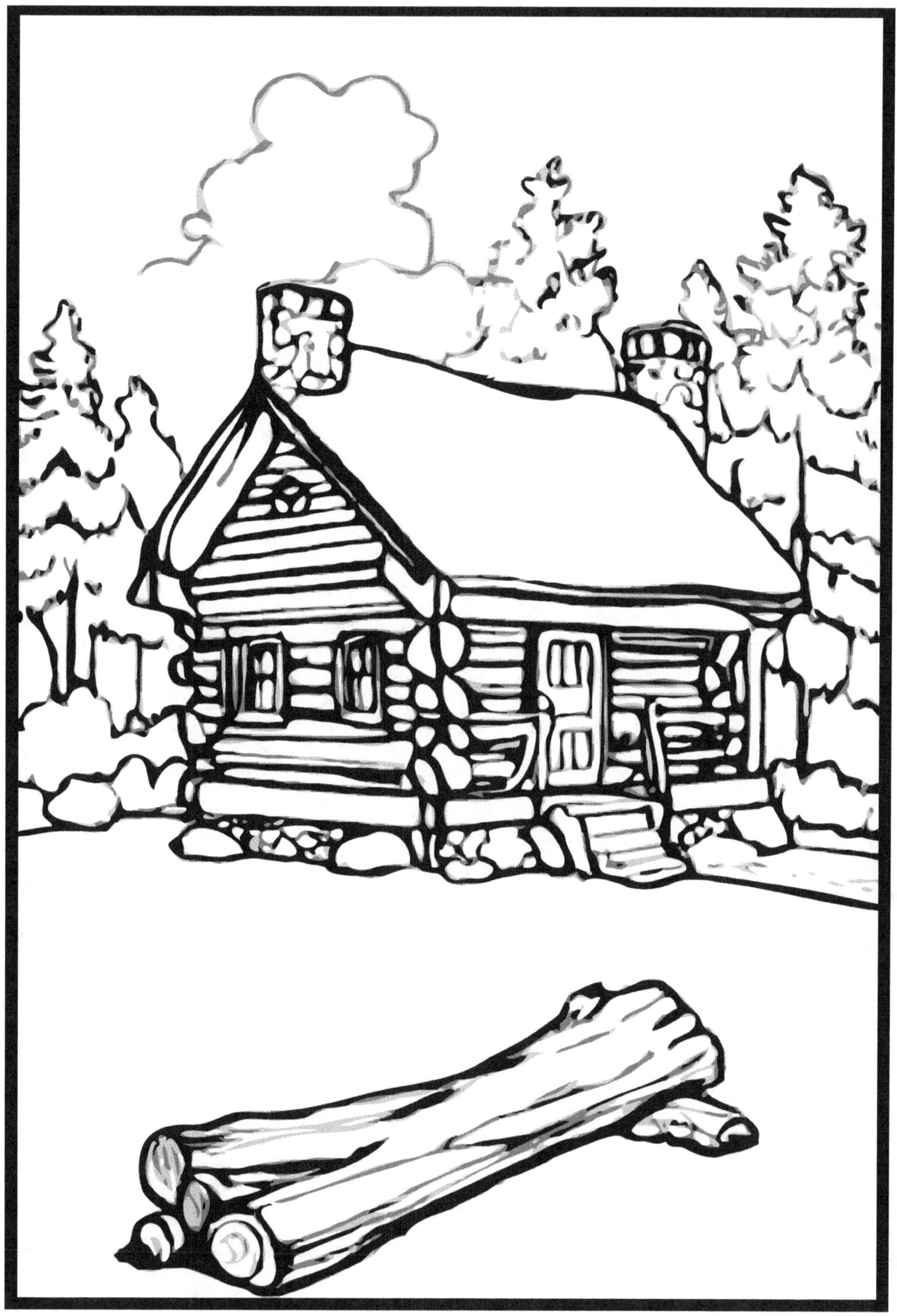

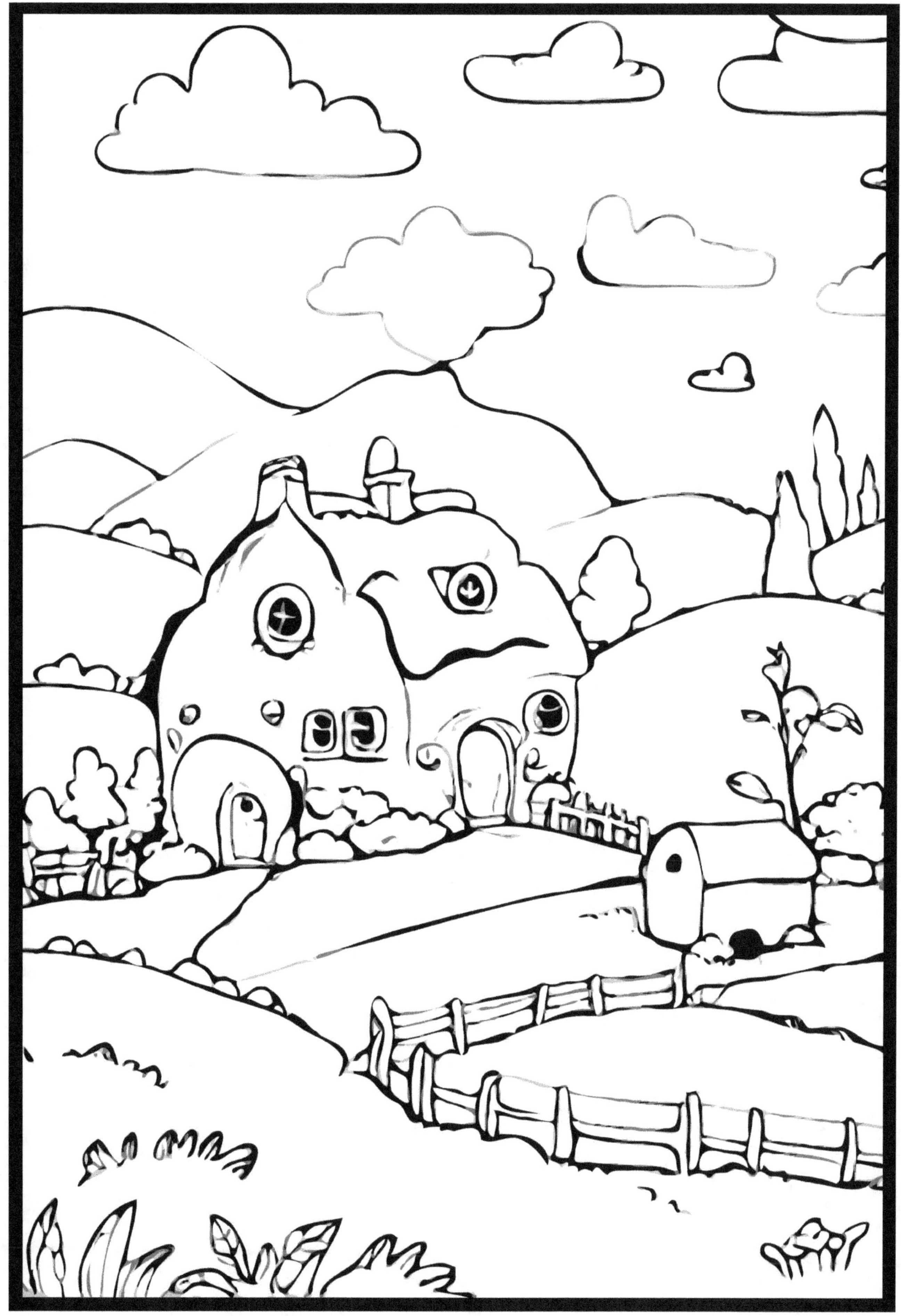

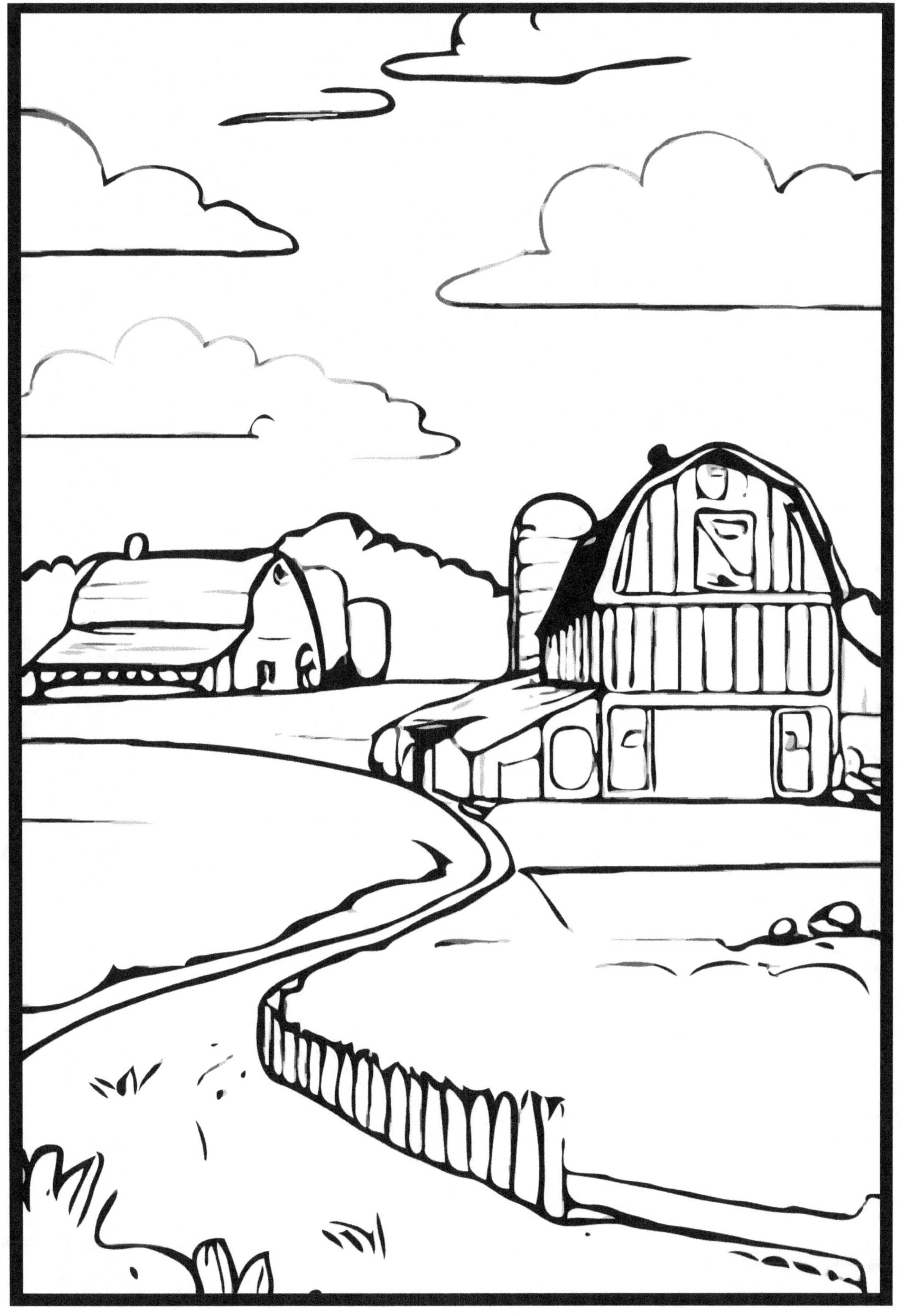

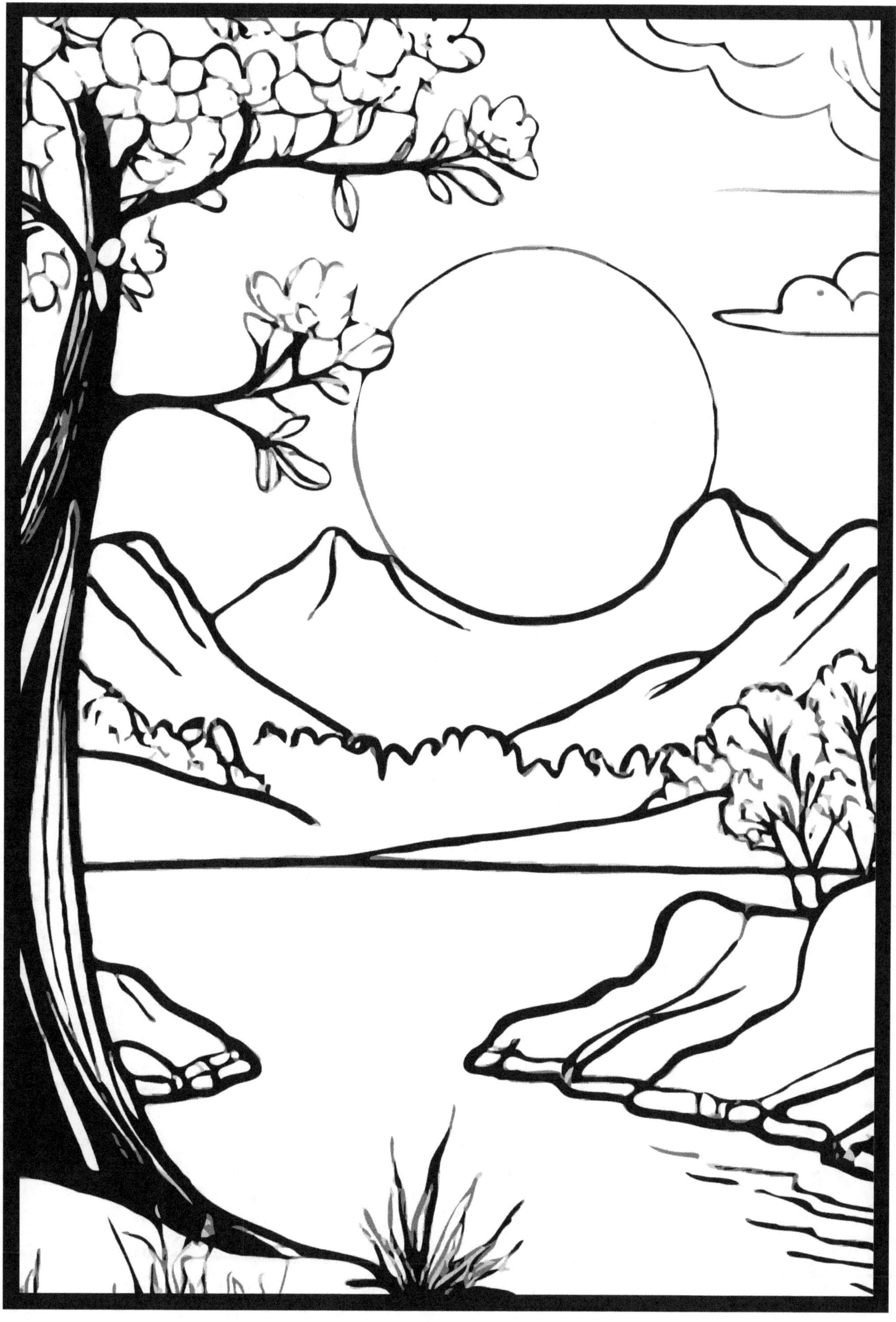

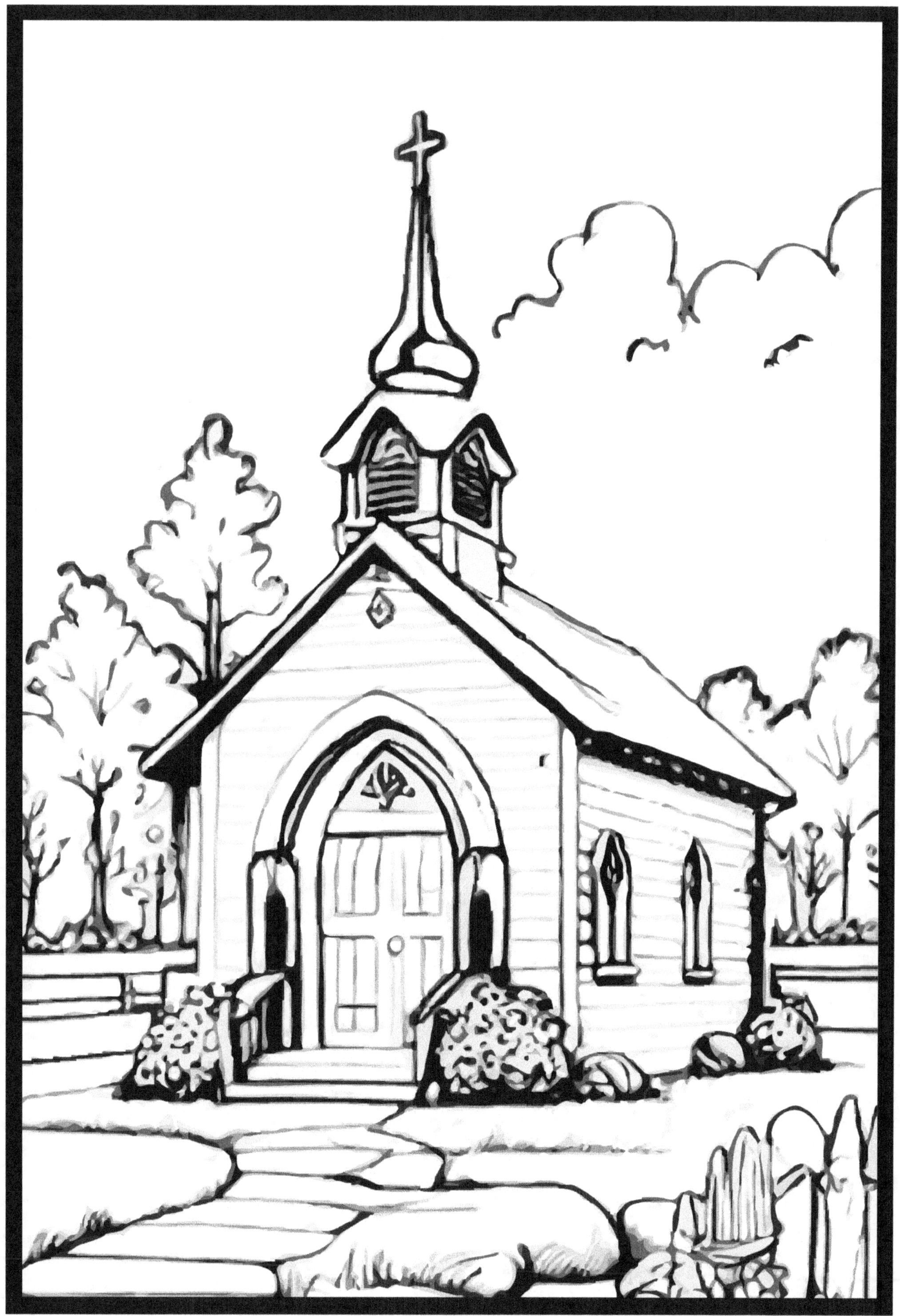

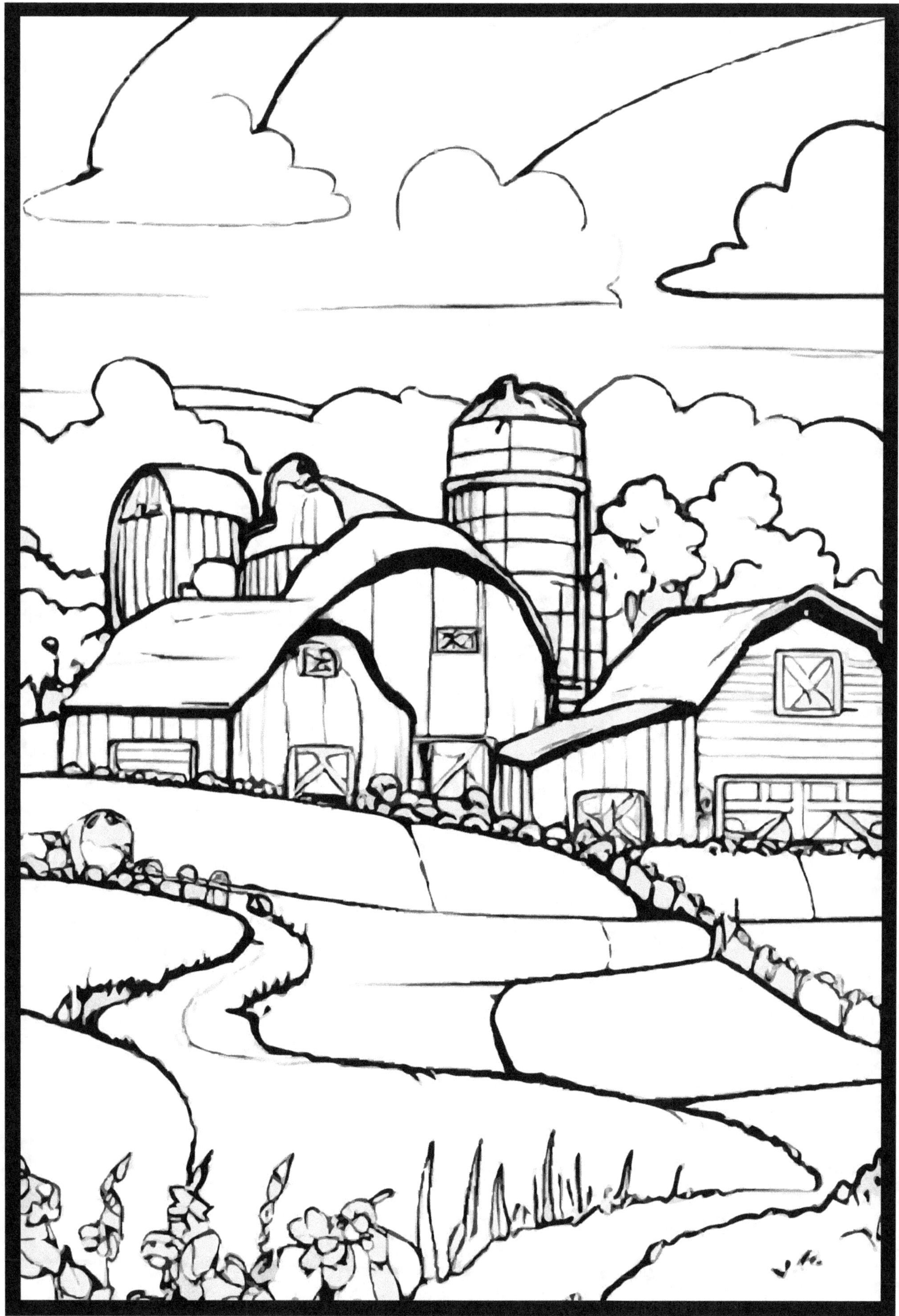

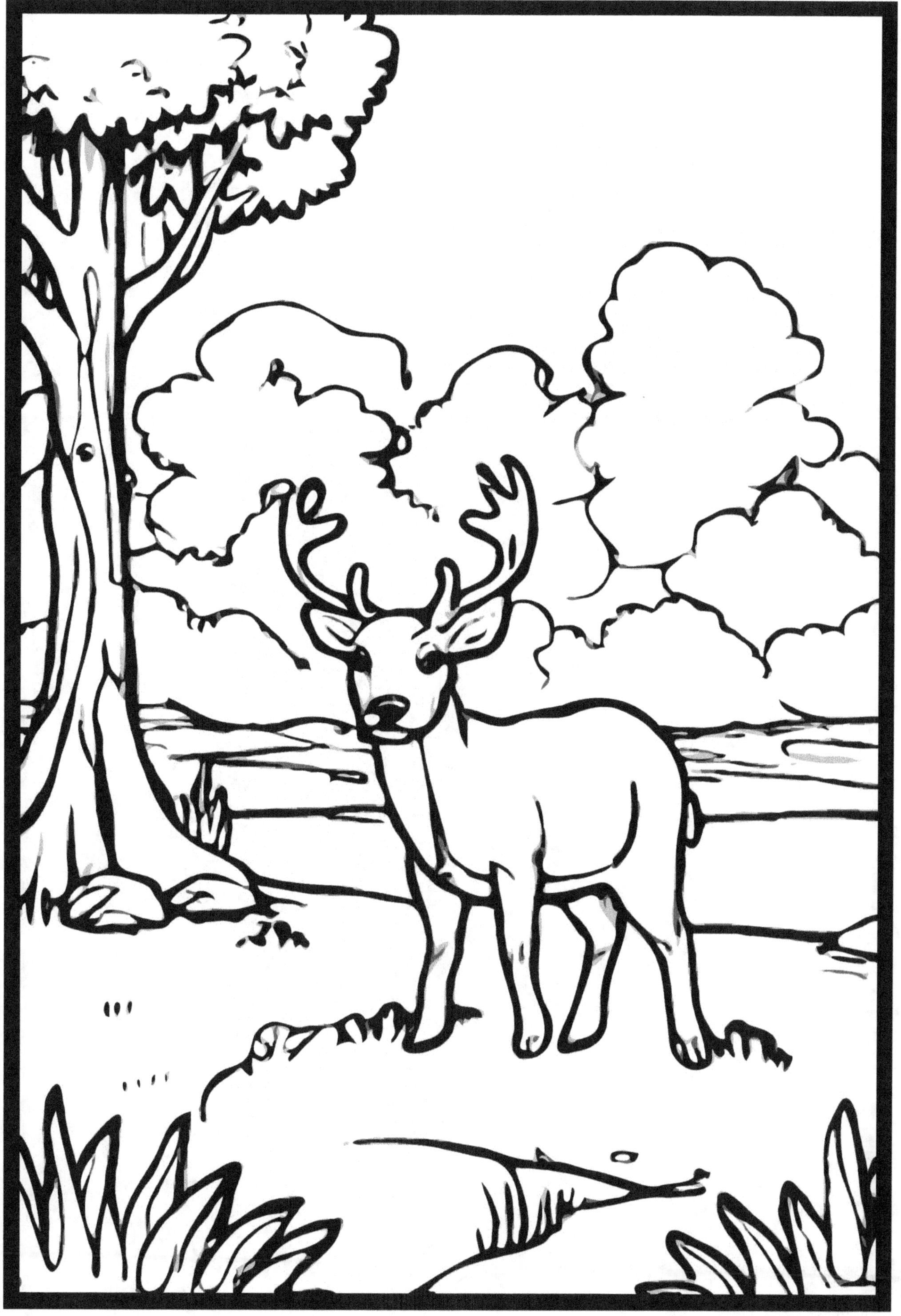